The
Decision-Making
Process for
Library Collections

Recent Titles in
Contributions in Librarianship and Information Science

The Decision-Making Process for Library Collections

Case Studies in Four Types of Libraries

BEATRICE KOVACS

Contributions in Librarianship and Information Science, Number 65
Paul Wasserman, Series Editor

GREENWOOD PRESS

New York · Westport, Connecticut · London

Library of Congress Cataloging-in-Publication Data

Kovacs, Beatrice.
    The decision-making process for library collections : case studies in
four types of libraries / Beatrice Kovacs.
        p.   cm.—(Contributions in librarianship and information
science, ISSN 0084-9243 ; no. 65)
    Includes bibliographical references.
    ISBN 0-313-26042-7 (lib. bdg. : alk. paper)
    1. Collection development (Libraries)—Decision making—Case
studies.   2. Library administration—Decision making—Case studies.
I. Title.   II. Series.
Z687.K68   1990
    025.2'1—dc20   89-26021

British Library Cataloguing in Publication Data is available.

Library of Congress Catalog Card Number: 89-26021
ISBN: 0-313-26042-7
ISSN: 0084-9243

First published in 1990

Greenwood Press, Inc.
88 Post Road West, Westport, Connecticut 06881

Printed in the United States of America

The paper used in this book complies with the
Permanent Paper Standard issued by the National
Information Standards Organization (Z39.48-1984).

10 9 8 7 6 5 4 3 2 1

To Helen Kovacs,
mother, mentor, friend, and outstanding librarian,
and to Lorand Kovacs,
wherever you are,
with love.

Contents

Part III: Conclusion

Part IV: Appendices

Illustrations

Preface

Over 10 years ago, I was given the responsibility of establishing a collection development program for a library that had been in existence for a century. Since there had never been a coordinated collection development program in this library, the collections were developed haphazardly.

This was the first time I was to create a coordinated program for collection development, although I had experience in selecting and purchasing materials for collections in several types of libraries. Therefore, as a first step, I reviewed relevant literature. I expected to find the collection development process described in the literature; instead, I found articles on whether to purchase from vendors or publishers, on the value of reviews and reviewing sources, and on how formulae were or were not helpful in a given library setting. There was a wealth of articles on mechanical methods of selecting, for example, given x number of students in y discipline then you should spend z percentage of your budget for relevant subjects. This was all very interesting, and occasionally helpful in identifying what did not work in certain situations. However, I could not find descriptions of how the experts developed a collection. By that I mean, what did those people who had years of experience in developing collections actually think? What information did they gather, and how did they gather it? What was helpful and what was irrelevant in the processes of deciding what to buy and how to spend funds for collections?

The purpose of this book is to identify, through one methodology, how some experienced selectors think when deciding to buy, not buy, or discard materials from their collections. It describes how experienced selectors in a variety of library settings develop collections and specifically how they think while selecting materials. This information was gathered over a period of six years in a series of research studies conducted in academic, public, school and special libraries. The data gathered, and discussion of selected new concepts, issues, and theories developed in the literature of librarianship, comprise the bulk of this book.

It is hoped that individuals entering the field of collection development and collection management will benefit by the experience of others, not only in understanding the theoretical framework but also in the day-to-day thinking processes and practical aspects of building collections. Experienced practitioners, on the other hand, may find that the information contained herein can supplement and augment the experience they have gained over the years. Often in the course of this research, volunteer selectors felt they might not have much to contribute because they "knew when something was right for the collections" based on some intuitive sense. It was through the prodding of their memories and the teasing of their subconscious thoughts that they were able to articulate decision-making processes that were, in fact, taking place. These processes had evolved over a period of time, eventually were ignored by the selectors, and became second nature to them. The selection process became "artistic," but artists need practice and training to hone their craft, and so do selectors.

This book is designed to help librarians identify the process of decision making. The fact that the decision-making process seems to be the same for all the selectors who participated in the research, regardless of the type of library in which they worked, is significant. While the subject areas or types of materials for which the selectors were responsible were vastly different, the ways in which they thought were very similar. In becoming aware of these decision-making processes, collection developers and collection managers can be more effective in their choice of materials. The possible ramifications of increased awareness include the ability to justify budgetary needs and expenditures, identify the appropriateness of the purchases for the collections, and defend against interference from censors who would shape collections to suit their personal beliefs.

This book would not have been possible without the unselfish participation of the volunteer selectors who gave many hours of their time during the interview process. Since they were promised anonymity, I cannot thank them by name, but they are all outstanding individuals who are "professionals" in every sense of the word.

I wish to thank the directors of the libraries, who allowed me to conduct the research in their libraries during the normal working hours for weeks at a time. Their generosity was matched by their interest in adding to the knowledge base of the profession.

Without the encouragement of Ellis Mount, I could not have attempted this work. As advisor and friend, he helped me see that this research should be shared with others. Without the support of my colleagues in the School of Education, and especially the Department of Library and Information Studies, of the University of North Carolina at Greensboro, the research could not have been completed. To Marilyn Miller, M. Sangster Parrott, Cora Paul Bomar, and Marilyn Shontz, special acknowledgment must be given. Also, thanks to the Public Library Section of the North Carolina Library Association for approving grant funding for the studies in public libraries through the Research Grant Program. Much of the information on school libraries could not have been included if it had not been for the careful research conducted by Bobbie M. Pell, author of Chapter 5. To David Purpel, who read this work and made excellent suggestions, thank you for your time and patience.

PART I
DECISION MAKING AND COLLECTION DEVELOPMENT

1

General Trends in Collection Development

It is both necessary and helpful to provide a historical context for the examination of current trends in collection development. Therefore, while this chapter is not intended to present the history of collection development in the United States, a summary of some important trends that have occurred over the years is presented as an introduction to the current state of librarianship.

From the first library collections, developed from personal collections of the educated gentry, through the library collections of today, there have been a number of issues facing those charged with the care and use of the materials. Some of these issues include:

- the debate over quality versus demand
- concern about the information explosion
- the problems with participation in interlibrary cooperation
- fiscal issues such as decreasing budgets and increasing costs

QUALITY VERSUS DEMAND

For example, the issue of quality versus demand has been debated for more than 50 years and there is still no consensus about it in the library profession.[1] Part of the problem may be that libraries, clientele, and information needs are too diverse. One language cannot be agreed upon for all the countries of the world. One religion is not appropriate for all the peoples of the world. One concept, either "demand" or "quality," is not valid for all the libraries either. One reason may be that a great deal depends on the goals and objectives of the library or information center.

Is the goal to provide materials to meet all the needs of the library's clientele? If so, then materials should be purchased for recreational as well as informational purposes. Recreational materials, such as popular fiction, may well fall into the category of "non-quality." On the other hand, informational materials are generally judged appropriate if experts have identified them as "quality" materials. These two concepts are not mutually exclusive. Demand materials may be, and often are, of quality, and vice versa. It is when demand materials are not deemed as being of quality that problems arise.

A possible resolution of the issue can be based on the type of library for which the collections are being built. The quality versus demand issue is most hotly debated in the public library sector. The goals and objectives of most public libraries are to provide what the community wants or needs. While selectors in public libraries tend to use their professional and educated judgment in purchasing nonfiction materials, they purchase fiction and recreational materials identified as appropriate through their contact with their clientele. There seems to be a double standard in public libraries, based on the purpose for which the material is designed. Certainly any public library that does not provide sufficient copies of current best sellers will lose support of the community when the patrons become frustrated in their attempt to get the books they desire. Public libraries must accede to the demands of the community. At the same time, the community might withdraw support from the library if the informational and factual materials are found to be lacking in quality. Community criticism is often centered on informational materials in the public library that are outdated or known to contain erroneous information.

At the other end of the spectrum is the special library. Created for a specific purpose, usually to provide accurate and current information for a particular set of patrons, the special library must contain materials considered to be of quality by those for whom it is designed. Inaccurate information in a special library may cause havoc for the supporting institution. For example, inaccurate patent information in a corporate library may lead to the loss of years of research and millions of dollars wasted on processes, procedures, and products that have already been licensed elsewhere. Law libraries that do not keep up with the most current legal activities in the country may jeopardize the life and freedom of clients. Health sciences libraries that do not provide access to the most current and accurate information for health care professionals may directly affect the health of the community and, potentially, of the nation. Newspaper and other media libraries, relied upon for accurate and quality information by reporters, could provide inaccurate information that may directly affect the well-being of citizens. These are just some of the examples of the need for quality in the special library collection.

School and academic libraries also face the problem of quality versus demand, but the issue is more clear-cut. School libraries are usually charged with the development of collections to support the curriculum, and materials for this purpose are identified by the faculty. Academic libraries, from junior colleges through universities, are also charged with supporting the curriculum, but with the additional charges to support any research needs of faculty, and to provide some recreational materials for students, faculty, and staff. While the mission and goals are clear, the materials needed to fulfill them are not as clearly defined.

THE INFORMATION EXPLOSION

Adding to the problem of "quality" materials versus materials in "demand" is the current and continuing phenomenon known as the "information explosion." As Evans points out, one of the special characteristics of information "is that it is neither scarce nor depleting. In fact, the more it is used and manipulated, the more information there is; many information problems are the result of too much information rather than too little."[2]

There have been many articles about the exponential growth of literature, particularly in the sciences, and the problems of libraries and information centers in trying to provide access to the information contained in this wealth of materials. At the same time, libraries have been trying to contend with the rising cost of this increased amount of materials, coupled with decreasing space in their physical facilities. There seems to be a "Catch 22" in the provision of information services in all types of libraries. More is being produced, of which more is desired for library collections, with decreased spending power in library budgets, and decreasing space available for housing that which is purchased.

Tied to the problems already mentioned is the set of issues created by the famous, or infamous, *Thor* tax ruling of 1979.[3] The press, and many authors in library literature,[4] predicted that this tax ruling would have a major impact on the acquisition of materials for library collections because publishers would produce shorter print runs of needed materials, and titles wanted by libraries would be declared out-of-print before purchase orders could be sent. An interesting analysis of the impact of the *Thor* tax ruling five years later was reported by Loe,[5] who surveyed publishers and academic acquisitions librarians regarding the effect of the ruling. Of the 85 publishers surveyed, 24 responses were usable with 50 percent of those indicating that their titles were not declared out-of-print faster in 1985 than in 1979, although 85 percent believed that "books in general were going O.P. faster now."[6] She sent 100 surveys to academic librarians and was able to include 66 responses in her tallies. A majority of the librarians (74 percent) noticed an increase in books going out-of-print before they could be acquired. Selectors in the humanities or mixed disciplines noticed this increase in out-of-print titles more than selectors in the sciences.[7]

If selectors and collection development librarians need to identify materials more quickly in order to purchase items before they are declared out-of-print, what sources of information are chosen to identify those materials? Each selector usually has some favorite sources, learned through experience as containing comprehensive, accurate listings of new materials. It seems that many sources geared to particular interests or types of collections are chosen by selectors for those collections. For example, many academic librarians name *Choice* as one of the selection tools from which they most successfully identify material for purchase. Public librarians often name *Booklist* and *Library Journal*. Special librarians often have specialized bibliographies providing information on new publications or productions available in the subject areas needed for their collections. School media center librarians rely on their professional journals and certain bibliographies, such as *Elementary School Library Collection*.[8]

At the same time, the impact of technology has created additional problems in accessing information. Not only are libraries and information centers trying to purchase relevant and appropriate print materials, but now they are also trying to provide information in alternative formats. Unfortunately, some of the new formats have not been developed according to any standards, and equipment purchased for access to one type of electronic information is useless for another. Examples of this problem include the commitment a library must make to MS-DOS, Apple, or CP/M computers and the purchase of programs for such operating systems, or the decision to buy equipment and cassettes for 1/2 inch, 3/4 inch, or 8mm videotapes.

The "High Sierra" standards[9] for compact laser disks are helpful in determining what equipment to buy for the current offerings of CD-ROM, but industry projections for the development of CD-I (compact disk-interactive) and other CD products in the near future[10] may make the current products obsolete. Should libraries commit funding and space for these current products, or wait to see what develops?

INTERLIBRARY COOPERATION

Perhaps the greatest impact on libraries caused by the improvements in technology is the ability to participate in electronic networks. Prior to the revolution in electronic communication, interlibrary cooperation consisted primarily of local area libraries agreeing to share collections and services. In some large metropolitan areas, telephone referral networks were attempted by special libraries, but they were not highly successful because of the lack of adequately trained personnel. Until the teletypewriter was put into use by many libraries in the 1950s, interlibrary loan requests were sent through the mails, causing delays in the receipt of materials from other libraries. Material likely to be needed by the library's patrons was purchased because delays of a few weeks for receipt of the items were not acceptable. The teletypewriter shortened the time taken for requesting and receiving materials, making interlibrary cooperation more attractive.

The development of on-line real-time computer communications, used by libraries to send a request and receive an answer in an instant, was an attractive alternative promoting interlibrary cooperation. Patrons could be assured that material was on its way and would be in hand in a short period of time.

The ability to provide inexpensive, permanent photocopies of requested materials also enhanced the opportunities for interlibrary cooperation after the resolution of the problems involving the violation of copyright laws. No longer did a library have to struggle with the dilemma of whether to send a bound copy of a periodical to a requesting library, or deny a request to a member of the network. A librarian simply photocopied the article and mailed it (although it is true that photographs and fine illustrations do not copy well).

The newest advances in technology are even more impressive. Now, a library can, with the right equipment, enter a request into a microcomputer and program that computer to send a request to another computer during inexpensive telephone line times (if possible). If both computers are attached to telefacsimile equipment, the lending library can send a copy of the material electronically in a matter of seconds. Recently, several authors have speculated on the future of library services based on this new technology.[11] However, the impact on the development of collections has not yet been determined because the technology is too new. Too few libraries at this time own and use the equipment, making it difficult to judge the effectiveness of this technology. There is the potential that the impact on collection development and collection management will be great because libraries can share material at little cost and less inconvenience than before.

FISCAL ISSUES

For a number of years libraries were the recipients of a great deal of funding from the federal government. The fifties and the sixties were times of plenty, with libraries receiving enough money from grants and budget supplements to purchase any material needed and to build facilties in order to house the increasing collections. Selectors planned purchasing programs on the basis of continuing support but were disappointed because, although library budgets remained stable, or increased with increments near or slightly above the cost of living, supplemental funding from the government decreased and prices for materials rose dramatically.[12] An analysis of the statistics recorded in *The Bowker Annual of Library and Book Trade Information* shows the publishing industry's escalation of the pricing structures for materials. Vendors have been frustrated in trying to provide efficient and cost-effective service as a liaison between the for-profit publisher and the not-for-profit library.[13]

Sensitivity of the publishing industry to the budget problems of libraries and information centers has varied over the years. Also, information that is manipulated and repackaged in electronic, un-copyrighted formats has become a problem. Some entrepreneurial publishers have been known to reprint public domain information and sell it for a price to buyers who, unaware that the material is in the public domain, order the titles. An example of such an occurrence was recorded in the *MLA News* for March 1982,[14] that warned medical librarians of a mental health directory, offered for sale by a publisher, that was an exact duplication of a free directory published by the Public Health Service.

SUMMARY

Quality versus demand, the information explosion, interlibrary cooperation, and money (or the lack of it) have been and continue to be the topics most often discussed in the literature on collection development. Interwoven within these topics are the newer concerns about technology and the impact on library collections and library services, and the patterns and problems of the publishing industry. Collection personnel must become well versed in all the new trends in order to anticipate the impact of those new trends on the information needs of their clientele. They must know about legislation, publishing, literature, economics, ethics, and almost everything else of interest to society.

In the past, libraries have depended on the need for services offered by the staff to justify their existence. This is no longer enough because for-profit information centers have been able to take a part of the information-seeker market and provide service for a fee. To survive, libraries and information centers should examine the gains made in the profit sector and apply any discoveries to the provision of library collections and service.

NOTES

1. G. Edward Evans, *Developing Library and Information Center Collections*, 2nd ed. (Littleton, CO: Libraries Unlimited, 1987), p. 82–95. Evans summarizes the differences in philosophy between Lionel McColvin, advocate of selection to meet demand, and Arthur Bostwick, Francis Drury, and Helen Haines, all of whom advocated selection of materials based on value to the collection or quality of the contents.

2. Evans, *Developing Library and Information Center Collections*, p. 2.

3. *Thor Power Tool Co. v. Commissioner of Internal Revenue* (439 U.S. 522–550), argued November 1, 1978, decided January 16, 1979 and implemented by the Internal Revenue Service in February 1980 (IRS ruling 0–60).

4. Ellen K. Coughlin, "IRS Ruling is Seen Threatening Supplies of Many Scholarly and Professional Books," *The Chronicle of Higher Education* 21 (September 29, 1980): 1, 22; Daniel N. Fischel, "Thor's Sledgehammer Blow Against Books . . . The Case for Repealing a Tax Law," *Publishers Weekly* 218 (August 1, 1980): 17–18; Robert Dahlin, "Thor: How Hard Will the Hammer Fall?" *Publishers Weekly* 218 (December 26, 1980): 28–32 and his "Learning to Live With Thor," *Publishers Weekly* 221 (March 5, 1982): 26–29; Evans, *Developing Library and Information Center Collections*, pp. 370–371; Karen A. Schmidt, " 'Never Read Any Book That Is Not a Year Old': Thor Power Tool, the Publishing Industry, and Library Collections," *Technical Services Quarterly* 2 (Spring/Summer 1985): 93–101; Leonard Schrift, "After Thor, What's Next: The Thor Power Tool Decision (US Supreme Court) and Its Impact on Scholarly Publishing," *Library Acquisitions: Practice and Theory* 9 (1985): 61–63; and various news articles and editorials in the professional literature during the years 1980 through 1984. Examples of such editorials include *Library Journal* 105 (October 1, 1980): 1999; *Newsletter on Intellectual Freedom* 30

(January 1981): 3–4; *Publishers Weekly* 222 (September 24, 1982): 25; *School Library Journal* 27 (November 1980): 9; *Top of the News* 37 (Winter 1981): 104–105; and *Wilson Library Bulletin* 55 (December 1980): 244.

5. Mary H. Loe, "*Thor* Tax Ruling After 5 Years: Its Effect on Publishing and Libraries," *Library Acquisitions: Practice & Theory* 10 (1986): 203–218.

6. Loe, "*Thor* Tax Ruling," p. 207.

7. Ibid., p. 211.

8. Lois Winkel, ed., *Elementary School Library Collection: A Guide to Books and Other Media*, 16th ed. (Williamsport, PA: Brodart, 1988).

9. High Sierra standards were produced by agreement of manufacturers of CD-ROM products during a meeting in 1987. It is interesting to note that in early 1989 a written copy of the standards could not be located. A call to the National Bureau of Standards produced the information that while such standards had been developed, no written copy was available, and some distributors of CD-ROM products stated that they were assured that their products conformed to the standards although they did not know what the standards were.

10. Laura Foti, "CD-I: A Focal Technology," *CD-ROM Librarian* 3 (May 1988): 21–24; Brian Nielsen, "The Second Annual CD-ROM Expo: The Latest in the Technology," *CD-ROM Librarian* 3 (November/December 1988): 14–18. For definitions of terms relating to optical technology, see Karen A. Becker, "CD-ROM: A Primer," *College & Research Libraries News* 48 (July/August 1987): 388–393.

11. Speculations about the electronic library and the impact of new technologies on libraries and collections include the following articles: Lawson Crowe and Susan H. Anthes, "The Academic Librarian and Information Technology: Ethical Issues," *Colleges & Research Libraries* 49 (March 1988): 123–130; David Farrell and Jutta Reed-Scott, "The North American Collections Inventory Project: Implications for the Future of Coordinated Management of Research Collections," *Library Resources & Technical Services* 33 (January 1989): 15–28; George R. Jaramillo, "Computer Technology and Its Impact on Collection Development," *Collection Management* 10 (1988): 1–13; F. W. Lancaster, "Electronic Publishing," *Library Trends* 37 (Winter 1989): 316–325; David W. Lewis, "Inventing the Electronic University," *College & Research Libraries* 49 (July 1988): 291–304; J. Newcomb, "Electronic Information Distribution: The Role of the Traditional Publisher and the Librarian," *Special Libraries* 74 (April 1983): 150–155; Meta Nissley, "Optical Technology: Considerations for Collection Development," *Library Acquisitions: Practice & Theory* 12 (1988): 11–15; Steven L. Sowell, "Expanding Horizons in Collection Development With Expert Systems: Development and Testing of a Demonstration Pro-

totype," *Special Libraries* 80 (Winter 1989): 45–50; Oldrich Standera, *The Electronic Era of Publishing: An Overview of Concepts, Technologies and Methods* (New York: Elsevier, 1987), pp. 257–259; and Erwin K. Welsch, "Back to the Future: A Personal Statement on Collection Development in an Information Culture," *Library Resources & Technical Services* 33 (January 1989): 29–36.

12. Chandler B. Grannis, "Book Title Output and Average Prices: 1987 Preliminary Figures," (pp. 402–412), and Rebecca T. Lenzini, "Prices of U.S. and Foreign Published Materials," (pp. 424–444), *The Bowker Annual of Library and Book Trade Information*, 33rd ed. (New York: Bowker, 1988); for a discussion of the problems publishers have with inflation and journal publishing, see Janet D. Bailey, "New Journal Decision Making," *College & Research Libraries* 50 (May 1989): 354–359.

13. Edward J. Lockman, "Is the Customer Always Right; or Wait a Minute, Don't You Want My Business? (Publishing Policies and Their Impact on Markets)," *Library Acquisitions: Practice & Theory* 11 (1987): 121–123.

14. "Librarians Beware!" *MLA News* 143 (March 1982): 5.

2

Decision Making in Collection Development Literature

"Research reveals that in fields other than library science, decision making has received and is receiving extensive consideration as a valuable key to sound, efficient, administrative activity."[1] In recent years, decision making has also come to the forefront in library science. A wealth of articles in the literature now address the process and practicality of using effective decision making to develop the services, collections, and activities that meet the needs of the clientele of various libraries and information centers.[2] It is interesting to note, however, that it has taken librarians a long time to recognize the value of the discoveries and developments in the for-profit sector of society.

Any discussion of the reasons for this delay in recognition would be unproductive speculation. Nevertheless, once the need for rational, reasonable, effective action is identified, and methodologies for developing these actions have been explained, it would be irresponsible for librarians to ignore this information. No longer do librarians enjoy the luxury of good to excellent financial support based on the premise that the provision of free library collections and information is a service vital to society. Accountability for expenditures is becoming more frequent.

On the other hand, there is the potential of becoming swept away in the tide of research methodology without having the opportunity to pause and reflect on the meaning of the methodological constructs on a given library situation. As stated by Hazen,

> we may find ourselves either condemned to broad and impressionistic historical surveys as our basis for planning and understanding, or consigned to abstruse statistical investigations of current reality with no clear understanding of the implications of any particular findings, or resigned to the elaboration of esoteric macro models of a complexity which defies either the cost rationality of their preparation, or any foreseeable practical application.[3]

BIBLIOMETRIC THEORIES

One of the ways in which librarians and information specialists try to develop objective accountability methodologies is through bibliometrics, the science or process of mathematically and statistically measuring the applicability of books or other materials to the collections of a library. To date, the majority of bibliometric theories that have been developed apply to academic or special library collections, perhaps because in those types of collections a specific subject focus is likely to be emphasized that could be quantitatively measured.

For example, Bensman[4] provides a readable analysis of the uses and value of bibliometrics in journal collection management in academic libraries. He summarizes the "laws" of bibliometrics, including:

- a relatively small proportion of a library's collection has concentrated usage;
- Bradford's "law of scattering," stating that articles on a scientific subject will appear not only in a core group of journals, but also in other journals;
- Garfield's "law of concentration," which refocuses Bradford's law to state that the literature of a discipline will include the core literature of other scientific disciplines.

Some methodologies attempt to identify the relevance or importance of existing collections by studying the circulation and in-house use of the materials. This enables researchers to develop theoretical frameworks regarding the expectation of use of future materials based on criteria common to materials used. Some researchers also project the value of this information to the allocation of resources, such as money, to areas of future use.[5] However, as Metz and Litchfield point out, "To some degree the use of any library collection must reflect the self-fulfillment of prophecies made by those who built the collection. Stated negatively, patrons cannot use materials the library never obtained."[6]

Citation Analyses

A familiar form of bibliometrics is citation analysis, about which much has been written, because the recent use of computers has enabled researchers to manipulate data in ways never before possible. A pioneer in citation analysis is Eugene Garfield, whose work at the Institute for Scientific Information has been the vanguard in mathematical and statistical analysis of the literature of science and technology.

A basic assumption in using citation analyis is that the frequency with which articles are cited indicates the importance of the articles to the discipline. Also, journals in which a majority of the cited articles appear are the most important or relevant journals in a subject field. These journals are assumed to contain the largest percentage of relevant articles to a subject,[7] although this assumption has been disputed by a number of authors.[8] Implications for collection development include the concept that the journals with articles most often cited are the journals that are most important to have in the library collection.

While citation analyses have been conducted primarily with periodical literature, the assumption can be made that equally valid results can be obtained by tracking monographic literature. Books that are most often cited by authors could be considered the most important books on the topic. In the sciences, however, monographic information usually appears too late to be of any assistance in collection development. By the time the information contained within the book has been published, it is usually out of date. By the time new authors cite this information, it is often too old. The value of this knowledge in the sciences is to identify books that have gained lasting value and should be retained, rather than discarded.

Applications of citation analysis to the humanities and social sciences are less frequent than in the sciences, and they seldom appear in the literature. Further research is needed, not only regarding scientific literature, but also the value of citation analysis in the other literatures and for other types of library situations. Consider Wiberley, who says,

> citation studies are no magic and foolproof mechanism for the selection of journals. But when considered in the context of other

standards and methods for selection, citation studies stand as a useful, if limited and imperfect, guide to the selection of the most important journals for a field.[9]

Formulas

A number of researchers and collection development personnel have developed formulas for the quantitative assessment of the materials selection process.

A "decision model for book acquisitions," developed by DePew,[10] assigns weights and values to a number of factors to assist acquisitions librarians in academic libraries to determine whether a book should be purchased or not. This model is designed to identify "whether it is more appropriate for the library to add a title, refer it to a cooperative group of libraries for possible acquisition, defer the decision, or drop the title altogether."[11]

Losee provides a "decision theoretic model" that offers methods for ranking books for selection, "using binary, Poisson, and normally distributed features."[12] This model is suggested for implementation "in a library where very large numbers of retrospective machine-readable catalog records are available containing information describing both books selected and books rejected."[13]

McInnis offers a method of using the Clapp-Jordan formula[14] for predicting the minimum adequate size in terms of volumes for academic libraries. He suggests implementing statistical regression analysis to estimate the values to assign to the elements of the equation.[15]

The complex mathematical calculations required to use some of these models would require an expertise and a time commitment that most collection developers or selectors do not have and could not afford. Nevertheless, as researchers and theorists continue to explore the possibilities of quantifying aspects of a qualitative job function, there is the possibility that easy-to-use and accurate formulaic methodologies will be developed in the near future. Certainly, many of the mathematical calculations can now be done by computers, providing the collection developer with information that was previously unavailable. Growing sophistication with quantitative methodologies tied to the analytical capabilities of the computer may yet produce tools for collection developers and selectors that can take much of the risk out of purchasing materials for libraries.

Book fund allocation formulas have been proposed for a number of decades. Sellen reviews the literature through 1985, summarizing the issues explored by authors in the development of such formulas for academic libraries.[16] In a thematic issue of *Library Acquisitions:*

Practice & Theory entitled "Formulas Revisited," a number of authors discuss current budget allocation formulas based on a variety of concerns in academic libraries.[17] The attractiveness of these formulas lies in the perception that an equitable method can be developed to expend limited budgets and still meet the needs of library users. Even the standards created by the Association of College and Research Libraries include formulas for assessing collections and allocating funds.[18] However, as Schad warns, "The inherent danger [with formulas] is that they can become a kind of quasi-fairness that is an end in itself."[19] The authors of an article on the problems that arose with the attempt to apply formulas in a college library point out that "rather than defend their allocation decisions with elaborate formulas (however well evolved), librarians instead need to be able to defend their decisions with their understanding of all the varied and sometimes ambiguous realities of the college library."[20]

While a majority of the articles discussing budget allocation formulas focus on problems in academic libraries, the literature does include suggested formulas for other types of libraries. For example, formulas for calculating budgetary needs for materials and equipment in school libraries and media centers appear in *Information Power: Guidelines for School Library Media Programs.*[21]

COLLECTION POLICIES

Most authors of literature on collection development agree that collection development policies are essential to the management of a collection development program. This concept is strengthened by the American Library Association's *Guidelines for Collection Development*, which states a number of assumptions, including that "a written collection development policy statement is for any library a desirable tool," and that the policy statement "can serve as both a planning tool and a communications device."[22]

The structure and content required in a model policy is, however, an area of disagreement for many authors, although a majority of the elements to be included is mentioned by most. Most authors agree that the mission and goals of the library and its sponsoring institution should be included, as well as statements on censorship and intellectual freedom.

In recent years it has been recommended that collection development policies also include listings of subject areas to be included in the collections and identification of the formats considered acceptable or desirable for the library's collections. More recently it has been suggested that the policy include statements of collection levels, to indicate the depth or intensity of collecting activity within each subject area.[23]

Of major impact in the literature of collection development policy construction, particularly in academic and research libraries, is the Research Libraries Group *Conspectus*. The *RLG Conspectus* is defined as "an overview, or summary, of existing collection strengths and future collecting intensities of RLG members," which is hoped to become "the cornerstone of a larger national cooperative effort."[24]

COLLECTION EVALUATION

The *Conspectus* is also one of the newest tools developed to aid in the analysis and evaluation of collections for research libraries. Collection evaluation has been attempted for many years, but efficient methods for conducting such evaluations were made possible only with the development and availability of computerized cataloging systems. Prior to the computer, collection evaluation was a time-intensive and labor-intensive activity that most libraries could not afford to undertake. The most common method for conducting collection evaluation, prior to the computer, was by checking lists, including "best books" lists, to ensure that the collection contained the most "valuable or important" books in a discipline. Now, a number of methodologies have been developed, using computers (and especially microcomputers), to assess the collection's relevance to the needs of the patrons and to the collection development policy.[25]

Mosher's review of collection evaluation[26] covers the literature through 1983. Since that time, a number of articles have been written that deal with newer methods or applications of evaluative systems, particularly as they relate to specific service areas or library job functions.[27]

One recent tool to aid in the evaluation of school library media center collections is the system called collection mapping, developed by David V. Loertscher.[28] This computerized mapping system is designed to identify the strengths of school library media collections and analyze the curriculum of the school, and compare the curriculum to the strengths of the collections. Then an acquisitions system is designed to match the collection map and an evaluation system measures the changes in the collection map from year to year.[29] While this system might not be appropriate for broad based general collections such as might be found in public or university libraries, the applicability of the concept for many special libraries should be explored.

SUMMARY

As can be seen through the literature, new technologies have enabled librarians and library researchers to develop new methods for gathering and analyzing data for collection development, evaluation, and assessment. Many authors present new and varied ways of collecting data and suggest methods of interpreting data to provide the basis for decision making. Literature describing the appropriate content of collection policies has identified components for the policies which, once developed, release the selector from having to make routine and repetitive decisions.

Few authors actually examine the decision-making process, the cognitive process of deciding what needs to be added to the collections. Rather, they discuss the data input and analysis as if by appropriately analyzing and evaluating the data, the decision process had been completed. There is, however, more to the decision-making process than collecting data and evaluating that data in terms of a specific framework.

NOTES

1. Theresa A. Goss, "Middle-Management Participatory Decision Making," *Community & Junior College Libraries* 3 (Fall 1984): 37.

2. Representative articles on effective decision making to develop services, collections, and activities in various libraries and information centers include: Jeffrey A. Raffel, "From Economic to Political Analysis of Library Decision Making," *College & Research Libraries* 35 (November 1974): 412–423; James C. Baughman, "Toward a Structural Approach to Collection Development," *College & Research Libraries* 38 (May 1977): 241–248; Arlene M. Feiner, "Frameworking in Cooperative Collection Development," *Illinois Libraries* 71 (January 1989): 25–31; Mary Sue Stephenson and Gary R. Purcell, "Application of Systems Analysis to Depository Library Decision Making Regarding the Use of New Technology," *Government Information Quarterly* 1 (1984): 285–307; and Gerald G. Hodges, "Decision-Making for Young Adult Services in Public Libraries," *Library Trends* 37 (Summer 1988): 106–114.

3. Dan C. Hazen, "Knowledge, Information Transactions, Collection Growth, and Model Building: Some Not-Quite-Random Thoughts," *Cornell University Library Bulletin* 212 (1979): 11–15.

4. Stephen J. Bensman, "Journal Collection Management as a Cumulative Advantage Process," *College & Research Libraries* 46 (January 1985): 13–29.

5. Some recent articles on collection use include Paul Metz and Charles A. Litchfield, "Measuring Collections Use at Virginia Tech," *College & Research Libraries* 49 (November 1988): 501–513; Tony Stankus and Barbara Rice, "Handle With Care: Use and Citation Data for Science Journal Management," *Collection Management* 4 (Spring/ Summer 1982): 95–110; F. W. Lancaster, "Evaluating Collections by Their Use," *Collection Management* 4 (Spring/Summer 1982): 15–43; and William E. McGrath, "Multidimensional Mapping of Book Circulation in a University Library," *College & Research Libraries* 42 (March 1983): 103–115.

6. Metz and Litchfield, "Measuring Collections Use," p. 510.

7. Robert N. Broadus, "A Proposed Method for Eliminating Titles From Periodical Subscription Lists," *College & Research Libraries* 46 (January 1985): 30–35; and his "On Citations, Uses, and Informed Guesswork: A Response to Line," *College & Research Libraries* 46 (January 1985): 38–39; Stephen E. Wiberley, Jr., "Journal Rankings From Citation Studies: A Comparison of National and Local Data From Social Work," *Library Quarterly* 52 (October 1982): 348–359.

8. Challenges to this theory include: Bert R. Boyce and Janet Sue Pollens, "Citation-Based Impact Measures and the Bradfordian Selection Criteria," *Collection Management* 4 (Fall 1982): 29–36; Maurice B. Line, "Use of Citation Data for Periodicals Control in Libraries: A Response to Broadus," *College & Research Libraries* 45 (January 1985): 36–37; and Stankus and Rice, "Handle With Care," (1982).

9. Wiberley, "Journal Rankings," p. 357–358.

10. John N. DePew, "An Acquisitions Decision Model for Academic Libraries," *Journal of the American Society for Information Science* 26 (July/August 1975): 237–246.

11. Ibid., p. 246.

12. Robert M. Losee, Jr., "A Decision Theoretic Model of Materials Selection for Acquisition," *Library Quarterly* 57 (July 1987): 269.

13. Ibid., p. 280.

14. Verner W. Clapp and Robert T. Jordan, "Quantitative Criteria for Adequacy of Academic Library Collections," *College & Research Libraries* 26 (September 1965): 371–380.

15. R. Marvin McInnis, "The Formula Approach to Library Size: An Empirical Study of Its Efficacy in Evaluating Research Libraries," *College & Research Libraries* 33 (May 1972): 190–198.

16. Mary Sellen, "Book Budget Formula Allocations: a Review Essay," *Collection Management* 9 (Winter 1987): 13–24.

17. The articles included in *Library Acquisitions: Practice & Theory*, volume 10, issue number 4 (1986) that are relevant to discussion concerning budget allocation formulas are: David C. Genaway, "PBA: Percentage Based Allocation for Acquisitions: A Simplified Method

for the Allocation of the Library Materials Budget" (pp. 287–292); David C. Genaway, "The Q Formula: The Flexible Formula for Library Acquisitions in Relation to the FTE Driven Formula" (pp. 293–306); Kent Mulliner, "The Acquisitions Allocation Formula at Ohio University" (pp. 315–327); with comments by Susan D. Jacobson (pp. 307–309) and Carol Wall (pp. 311–313).

18. A list of the standards and guidelines for a variety of academic libraries, including colleges, universities, and junior colleges, can be obtained from the ACRL/ALA, 50 East Huron Street, Chicago, IL 60611 or can be found in issues of *College & Research Libraries News*.

19. Jasper G. Shad, "Fairness in Book Fund Allocation," *College & Research Libraries* 48 (November 1987): 484.

20. Dorothy C. Senghas and Edward A. Warro, "Book Allocations: The Key to a Plan for Collection Development," *Library Acquisitions: Practice and Theory* 6 (1982): 50.

21. "Appendix B: Budget Formulas for Materials and Equipment," in: American Association of School Librarians and Association for Educational Communications and Technology, *Information Power: Guidelines for School Library Media Programs*, (Chicago: American Library Association, 1988), pp. 124–130.

22. American Library Association, *Guidelines for Collection Development*. (Chicago: American Library Association, 1979).

23. A clear and readable description of the concept of collection levels appears in Ross Atkinson, "The Language of the Levels: Reflections on the Communication of Collection Development Policy," *College & Research Libraries* 47 (March 1986): 140–149. An example of the development of a collection development policy for one university library is described by Elliot Palais, "Use of Course Analysis in Compiling a Collection Development Policy Statement for a University Library," *Journal of Academic Librarianship* 13 (1987): 8–13.

24. Nancy E. Gwinn and Paul H. Mosher, "Coordinating Collection Development: The RLG Conspectus," *College & Research Libraries* 44 (March 1980): 128–140. Two examples of articles describing the creation of collection development policy that include the *RLG Conspectus* are Mary J. Bostic, "A Written Collection Development Policy: To Have and Have Not," *Collection Management* 10 (1988): 89–103; and Edward Lein, "Suggestions for Formulating Collection Development Policy Statements for Music Score Collections in Academic Libraries," *Collection Management* 9 (Winter 1987): 69–89. Other articles about the uses of the *RLG Conspectus* include Anthony W. Ferguson, Joan Grant, and Joel S. Rutstein, "The RLG Conspectus: Its Uses and Benefits," *College & Research Libraries* 49 (May 1988): 197–206; Christopher A. Millson-Martula, "The Greater Midwest Regional Medical Library Network and Coordinated Collection Development:

The RLG Conspectus and Beyond," *Illinois Libraries* 71 (January 1989): 31–39; and Larry R. Oberg, "Evaluating the Conspectus Approach for Smaller Library Collections," *College & Research Libraries* 49 (May 1988): 187–196.

25. One example of an article describing a collection evaluation method requiring computer analysis is Mark Sandler's, "Quantitative Approaches to Qualitative Collection Assessment," *Collection Building* 8 (1988): 12–17.

26. Paul H. Mosher, "Quality and Library Collections: New Directions in Research and Practice in Collection Evaluation," *Advances in Librarianship* 13 (1984): 211–238.

27. Examples of such articles include Sheila S. Intner, "Responsibilities of Technical Service Librarians to the Process of Collection Evaluation," *Library Trends* 22 (Winter 1985): 417–436; Peter G. Watson, "Collection Development and Evaluation in Reference and Adult Services Librarianship," *RQ* 26 (Winter 1986): 143–145; and Nancy P. Sanders, Edward T. O'Neill, and Stuart L. Weibel, "Automated Collection Analysis Using the OCLC and RLG Bibliographic Databases," *College & Research Libraries* 49 (July 1988): 305–314.

28. David V. Loertscher, "The Elephant Technique of Collection Development," *Collection Management* 7 (Fall/Winter 1985/86): 45–54; David V. Loertscher, "Collection Mapping: An Evaluation Strategy for Collection Development," *Drexel Library Quarterly* 21 (Spring 1985): 9–21. An article describing the use of this collection mapping technique is William Murray et al., "Collection Mapping and Collection Development," *Drexel Library Quarterly* 21 (Spring 1985): 40–51.

29. David V. Loertscher and May Lein Ho, *Computerized Collection Development for School Library Media Centers.* School Library Media Programs, No. 20 (Fayetteville, AK: Hi Willow Research and Publishing, P.O. Box 1801, Fayetteville, AK 72702-1801, 1986).

3

Some Decision-Making Theories in Organizational Administration

Many authors writing in the areas of organizational diagnosis and administrative behavior have discussed the theory and practice of decision making.[1] There is considerable disparity in the theories offered by these authors and some disagreement about the way in which decisions are made. An examination of some of these theories and practices will help to identify those that could be applicable to the process of decision making in libraries.

Herbert A. Simon wrote,

> Although any practical activity involves both "deciding" and "doing," it has not commonly been recognized that a theory of administration should be concerned with the processes of decision as well as with the processes of action. This neglect perhaps stems from the notion that decision-making is confined to the formulation of over-all policy. On the contrary, the process of decision does not come to an end when the general purpose of an organization has been determined.[2]

Although the goals, mission, and objectives of the library may have been determined previously by either the library administration or by another governing body, the growth and direction of the library collection involve a constant stream of daily decisions that require the recognition of a number of factors before selections for the collections can be made.

Simon describes behavior as involving both unconscious and conscious selection of particular actions: unconscious actions are those which are developed as reflex, such as a typist using the "touch method" (called programmed decisions by Leigh[3]); and conscious actions are those in which selection is the product of a complex chain of activities called "planning" or "design" activities.[4] The conscious actions are those that can and should be analyzed when identifying the processes used in decision making for collection development in libraries.

A definition of *decision* is in order here. Accepting the idea that there are unconscious and conscious actions, it then follows that the conscious actions can be directed to beneficial or appropriate channels. This direction usually involves a decision. A *decision*, as defined by Mintzberg, Raisinghani, and Théorêt, is "a specific commitment to action (usually a commitment of resources)." They continue with the *decision process*, defining it "as a set of actions and dynamic factors that begins with the identification of a stimulus for action and ends with the specific commitment to action."[5]

The decision process is not easily identifiable, and many authors have developed structures for the process that are in many ways similar, yet differ in important points. For example, Heirs and Pehrson describe "four clearly definable stages in the . . . thought process of decision making":

1. formulating a question to be answered

2. gathering information in order to identify and/or create alternative answers to the question

3. predicting the consequences of acting on each of the alternative answers

4. making a judgment/decision by selecting what appears to be the best alternative answer to the question[6]

McCall and Kaplan describe four "elements" of the decision process, which are usually present but are not clear, separate stages nor appear in any order:

1. recognizing and defining problems

2. selecting certain problems for action

3. acting on problems (from quick decisions to convoluted processes)
4. interpreting the consequences of action[7]

Wheeler and Janis identify five stages:

1. accepting the challenge
2. searching for alternatives
3. evaluating alternatives
4. becoming committed (to a new course of action)
5. adhering to the decision[8]

Raiffa, in discussing the analysis of a decision problem, says that one must,

1. list the viable options available to you for gathering information, for experimentation, and for action
2. list the events that may possibly occur
3. arrange in chronological order the information you may acquire and the choices you may make as time goes on
4. decide how well you like the consequences that result from the various courses of action open to you
5. judge what the chances are that any particular uncertain event will occur[9]

Archer discovered through an extensive study of the decision processes of managers, supervisors, and executives that he could identify a nine-phase process, with the following sequence:

1. monitor the decision environment
2. define the decision problem or situation
3. specify the decision objectives
4. diagnose the problem or situation
5. develop alternative solutions or courses of action
6. establish the methodology or criteria for appraising alternatives
7. appraise alternative solutions or courses of action
8. choose the best alternative solution or course of action
9. implement the best alternative solution or course of action[10]

Mintzberg analyzes the decision process and names seven "routines" that describe the steps involved in decision making: recognition, diagnosis, search, design, screening, evaluation/choice, and authorization.[11]

Mintzberg, Raisinghani, and Théorêt discuss these decision processes in terms of "unstructured" decision processes "that have not been encountered in quite the same form and for which no predetermined and explicit set of ordered responses exists in the organization," and "strategic" processes, which are "important, in terms of the actions taken, the resources committed, or the precedents set."[12]

Gordon, Miller, and Mintzberg add another dimension to this discussion by defining the term *decision model* as "a decision process that is reasonably well-defined (outside the brain of the decision-maker, e.g., in flowchart form, in mathematical notation, on paper, or in a computer memory)."[13] A variety of decision models exist in the literature, including decision trees, decision tables, and decision flowcharts.[14]

In addition, there is the consideration of what Mintzberg identifies as "dynamic factors," which are of importance to decision making. He states, "Strategic decision-making processes are stopped by interruptions, delayed and speeded up by timing factors, and forced to branch and cycle. These processes are, therefore, dynamic ones of importance. Yet it is the dynamic factors that the ordered, sequential techniques of analysis are least able to handle. Thus, despite their importance, the dynamic factors go virtually without mention in the literature of management science."[15]

The more detailed routines identified by Mintzberg[16] and expanded by Mintzberg, Raisinghani, and Théorêt,[17] seem conducive to the study of collection development in libraries and are used as the framework for this study of the decision-making process, in conjunction with identification, as far as possible, of the dynamic factors influencing the decision-making process. These routines and dynamic factors are certainly important in the decision-making process in collection development as well as in business administration, and yet they go unmentioned in the literature of librarianship.

In addition to individual behavior as discussed by Simon, and the routines and dynamic factors discussed by Mintzberg, there are structural levels in the formal authority relationships within an organization, such as those discussed by Arlyn Melcher.[18] These structural levels for decision making include extensive discretion, in which individuals have broad discretion in making decisions; moderate discretion, in which policy and procedure statements and rules cover most of the important decisions; and restricted discretion, in which policies, procedures, and rules limit discretion in the decision-making process to routine details. In the development of collections, it would be of value to be able to determine the levels of discretion that the selectors are given, in order to study the effectiveness of their decision making in their library's collection development programs.

Since collections in libraries play such an important part in the information exchange process, analysis of decision making in collection development is a very important area for study in librarianship. With a better understanding of decision making and the influence of such factors as the "information explosion," rising costs for materials, concern for quality information resources, interlibrary cooperation, and decreasing or static budgets, librarians can improve the design of their collection development programs and create a solid framework for collection building to meet the needs of their clientele.

A research design formulated to examine the on-going decision-making process of collection development personnel in a variety of types of libraries[19] revealed the routines, dynamic factors, and structural levels influencing their decision process. For the creation of this research design, two assumptions were made. It was assumed that there is a wealth of material both in subject matter and by format to meet the informational needs of the library clientele, and there is appropriate and ready access through a variety of sources to the material that meets the informational needs of the library clientele.

In an attempt to identify the process of decision making done by collection development personnel, the investigator asked each selector to be aware of his or her thoughts throughout the study period and to identify those thoughts during weekly interview sessions. The responses of the selectors were then analyzed in terms of the framework for the steps in the decision-making process identified by Mintzberg.[20]

STEPS IN THE DECISION PROCESS

Routine 1: Recognition

There are several phases to the recognition routine. For example, the selector may have recognized that there is a need for greater coverage of a particular subject area in the collection or a user may have brought to the attention of the selector a title that was available and that would be of value in the collections. New programs, new areas of interest to the institution, or new groups of patrons that were identified for service were stimuli for selectors in identifying materials for purchase. The selectors expressed a concern for and a knowledge of the collections within the library, which kept them apprised of new materials that would enhance the usefulness of the library to the clientele or institution. Therefore, most selectors continually scanned the published literature and advertisements to stay aware of current trends and identify items for purchase for the library's collections. The following are descriptions of the methods in which selectors recognized the needs of their libraries.

Public Libraries. During the period studied, selectors in the four public libraries identified patron requests as the most frequent method for recognizing titles needed for the collections. Other methods by which needs or titles were recognized, in order of frequency, were:

- new materials listed in standard reviewing sources, publisher's advertising, and newspapers or television programs
- new editions of reference or popular materials
- replacements for missing or damaged material
- upcoming events such as science fairs, summer reading programs, essay contests, and class assignments in local schools
- materials listed in special bibliographies
- subject gaps in the collections found while aiding patrons
- recommendations made by colleagues
- buying trips to bookstores, in and out of town
- target areas identified through collection evaluation
- publications by local authors

School Libraries. The librarians indicated that requests from school faculty, library faculty, school staff, students, and parents were the primary ways in which they identified materials for purchase.

Academic Libraries. Faculty and student requests were mentioned by all selectors as the main way in which they recognized the need for purchase. Also identified were:

- new materials listed in standard reviewing sources, publisher's advertising, and special publisher or vendor sales
- interlibrary loan request analysis
- replacements for missing or damaged materials
- specialized bibliographies
- subject gaps, or imbalance, in collections found during research by faculty or students
- new courses proposed in their institutions
- approval plan books

- evaluation of general areas of the collections
- materials of local interest
- identification of new academic majors

Special Libraries. Once again, requests from patrons were the most common means by which selectors recognized the need for materials. In addition, the following, in order of frequency, were listed by the selectors as ways in which they identified needs or titles for the collections:

- interlibrary loan request analysis
- new courses proposed in their institutions
- reading lists for existing courses
- faculty publications
- requests for reserve materials
- replacements for worn or missing materials
- accreditation team site visits

Routine 2: Diagnosis

In every case, the selectors, having recognized a need for a subject or title within the collections, determined what characteristics would be necessary to fulfill that need. This was the diagnosis stage of the decision-making process. Following criteria that had been developed over a period of time, they identified the characteristics of the items that would be acceptable in materials purchased for the collections, such as language of publication, date of publication, copyright date, format, price, and so on. In libraries with collection development policies, these criteria were most often included in the policies and aided the selectors in deciding what was needed.

Routine 3: Search

When titles were recommended to or identified by selectors during the recognition and diagnosis routines, the search routine consisted of checking catalogs of the collections to determine whether the item was already owned by the library or of checking the on-order files to see if it was on order.

If need for materials was determined and no titles were brought to the attention of the selectors, a search was instituted for material that would fulfill the needs identified. All selectors had favorite sources that were examined to identify titles that filled the criteria developed in Routine 2, and those titles that met the requirements were then examined in terms of the search routine used for requested titles.

Selectors were asked to keep in mind the reasons why they did not select many of the potential titles during the study period, in order to identify their thoughts during the search process. The following list includes all reasons given by selectors for deciding to not purchase materials.

Subject coverage
- out-of-scope subject coverage
- out-of-date publication date
- duplication of subject coverage in the collections
- too elementary or too scholarly
- too specialized, technical, or esoteric
- subject treatment not appropriate to age level
- poorly or inappropriately presented
- no demand for the subject

Cost
- too expensive
- too close to encumbering entire budget
- subject allocation already spent

Format
- inappropriate for the collection
- inappropriate for the subject matter

Other
- negative reviews
- poor publisher reputation
- does not fit stated criteria for purchase
- inappropriate foreign language
- likelihood of availability on interlibrary loan
- expectation of lack of use

Routine 4: Design

In terms of decision making for collection development for libraries, this routine can be applied to the method determined most effective for the procurement of the information necessary to fulfill the needs identified earlier. For example, it may be determined that a particular title could meet a particular need or use but that it would be a short-term need that may not require the expenditure of funds to purchase the item. Since the item may be available on interlibrary loan from another institution, the selector may recommend that the requestor obtain the item through the interlibrary loan system. If the selector determined that the title would be of value to the collection, then the design would involve the determination of the best method of purchasing the item, including choice of vendor or supplier for the item.

Routine 5: Screening

If the title is to be purchased for the collection, and alternative sources for acquisition have been identified, those sources are screened to find which source could produce the title most effectively. For example, if it is necessary to produce the item for the user in the shortest time possible, and the title is located in a local bookstore, the selector may decide to purchase the title at the bookstore and have it picked up immediately. In another case, the selector may determine that speed is not of the essence and that a discount that may be offered by a supplier is of more value to the library even though several weeks may pass before the title is received. Vendor or supplier reputation for accuracy, speed, and service play a great part in the screening process; the selectors expressed awareness and concern with the effectiveness of vendors and suppliers to fulfill orders quickly and accurately.

Routine 6: Evaluation/Choice

The title that would fulfill a need was identified, and a vendor or supplier was chosen from which to purchase that title. All the pertinent information was gathered as to the availability of that title, including cost. The selectors once again examined all the information and decided whether or not to purchase the title. Most of the selectors expressed that they occasionally had second thoughts about materials they had originally decided to purchase; they sometimes changed their minds and did not order the items.

Routine 7: Authorization

If the title was recommended for purchase, the selector then completed the decision process by authorizing the title for purchase. This step took various forms in the libraries. In some libraries, titles were sent to the Technical Services or Acquisitions Department personnel for ordering. In others, recommendations were sent to the selector's department chair for review before order or selectors were responsible for creating and sending orders for materials without review by others.

The collection development and acquisitions processes in all types of libraries can be analyzed in terms of the decision-making processes described in the literature of organizational analysis. With such analysis, it is possible to study how the decisions were made to identify and purchase materials for collections.

The method in which the decisions are made is not the only aspect of decision making that needs to be analyzed. In addition, there are dynamic factors such as timing problems and interruptions that influence the decision-making process.

DYNAMIC FACTORS IN THE DECISION-MAKING PROCESS

As stated by Mintzberg, "Strategic decision-making processes are stopped by interruptions, delayed and speeded up by timing factors, and forced repeatedly to branch and cycle. These processes are, therefore, dynamic ones of importance."[21] What are the dynamic factors that influenced the decision-making processes of the selectors in the four libraries? Six groups of dynamic factors, identified by Mintzberg, Raisinghani, and Théorêt,[22] are used to describe the factors generally occurring in the decision-making process of individuals in the corporate world:

interrupts: when environmental factors and sudden events interrupted the decision process and caused changes in pace or direction;

scheduling delays: developed by decision makers to allow complex decisions to be made in manageable steps, so that the decisions can be integrated with other tasks;

feedback delays: generally occur when the decision maker awaits the results of a previous action;

timing delays and speedups: decision makers may purposely speed up or delay a decision process to take advantage of special circumstances, to await support or better conditions, etc., to facilitate smooth execution of the decision;

comprehension cycles: factors that cause the decision process to cycle back to an earlier phase; and

failure recycles: when the decision process has no acceptable solution, the decision maker may delay the decision until an acceptable solution can be found, or until the criteria can be changed.

Application of this framework to the decision-making processes of the selectors in this study is discussed in detail in Chapter 9.

STRUCTURAL LEVELS OF DISCRETION

There are structural levels in the formal authority relationships within an organization. These structural levels in decision making, as described by Melcher[23] and adopted for these studies, are identified as extensive discretion, moderate discretion, and restricted discretion.

Levels of discretion in the decision-making process may have an important influence on selection for the library's collection. These levels were used to determine whether discretionary freedom or discretionary restrictions had any impact on the collection development programs of the libraries under study.

Extensive Discretion. Individuals with extensive discretion have full and final authority in the purchase of materials. They are accountable only to the governing authority of the library.

Moderate Discretion. Selectors with moderate discretion have some authority to purchase materials but are accountable to a supervisor. Their decisions are governed by policy and procedure statements and their most important decisions must be in accord with rules developed for the library.

Restricted Discretion. Policies, procedures, and rules limit the discretion in the decision-making process to routine details. The selectors should not deviate from the rules in acquiring materials for the collections. Generally, all decisions must be approved by a supervisor.

Most selectors participating in this research had moderate or extensive discretion in their decision making regarding the purchase of materials for the collections. Those with extensive discretion could not identify any instances when items they chose for purchase were not acquired. Selectors with moderate discretion felt few, if any, constraints on their choices. Their recommendations were purchased in most cases.

Selectors with restricted discretion also felt that most of their recommended titles were purchased. Only in cases where there was no feedback built into the library's ordering mechanism were the selectors unable to determine whether everything they requested was actually purchased. This was true not only for those with restricted discretion, but also for those with moderate or extensive discretion.

In many cases, the selectors did not know whether materials they ordered had arrived, or had actually been ordered, or were not on order because they were no longer available (i.e., out-of-stock, out-of-print, or never printed). Most selectors did not keep a file of the titles they ordered; they simply forwarded recommendations to the appropriate individual. With no individual files and a lack of feedback, some selectors ordered the same title two or more times because it was mentioned in several of the sources they regularly scanned and they were unaware of their previous order recommendations. This, naturally, increased the workload of others in the library who had the responsibility for pre-order searching.

SUMMARY

The decision-making process is complex and can be interpreted in various ways. A number of theorists have developed matrices to analyze the decision process. Many of these matrices can be applied to decision making done by selectors in libraries. Mintzberg's matrix was chosen because it seemed to be most readily adaptable to the types of decisions made by selectors in libraries. In addition to the matrix, other factors are identified that impact the decision process and must be studied, including dynamic factors that may affect the decisions and the levels of discretion permitted selectors in the library.

All of these facets must be analyzed in terms of the setting in which the decision maker works. In order to understand the process used by the selectors in these studies, brief descriptions of the libraries in which they work are given in Chapters 4 through 7.

NOTES

1. A readable summary of much of the decision-making literature is Andrew Leigh's *Decisions, Decisions! A Practical Management Guide to Problem Solving and Decision Making* (Brookfield, VT: Gower Publishing Co., 1983).

2. Herbert A. Simon, *Administrative Behavior: A Study of Decision-Making Process in Administrative Organization*, 3rd ed. (New York: Free Press, 1976), p. 1.

3. Leigh, *Decisions, Decisions!*, p. 37.

4. Simon, *Administrative Behavior*, p. 3.

5. Henry Mintzberg, Duru Raisinghani, and André Théorêt, "The Structure of 'Unstructured' Decision Processes," *Administrative Science Quarterly* 21 (June 1976): 246. These ideas are also expressed by Bernard M. Bass, *Organizational Decision Making* (Homewood, IL: Richard D. Irwin, 1983), p. 3, when he says, "Decisions are action oriented. They are judgments which directly affect a course of action. But the decision process involves both thought and action culminating in an act of choice."

6. Ben Heirs and Gordon Pehrson, *The Mind of the Organization: On the Relevance of the Decision-Thinking Processes of the Human Mind to the Decision-Thinking Processes of Organizations* (New York: Harper & Row, 1972), pp. 9–10. This list was subsequently explained in more detail in Ben Heirs, with Peter Farrell, *The Professional Decision-Thinker: Our New Management Priority* (London: Sidgwick & Jackson, 1986), p. 27–29.

7. Morgan W. McCall, Jr. and Robert E. Kaplan, *Whatever It Takes: Decision Makers At Work* (Englewood Cliffs, NJ: Prentice-Hall, 1985), p. 105.

8. Daniel D. Wheeler and Irving L. Janis, *A Practical Guide for Making Decisions* (New York: Free Press, 1980), pp. 6–9.

9. Howard Raiffa, *Decision Analysis: Introductory Lectures on Choices Under Uncertainty* (Reading, MA: Addison- Wesley, 1968), pp. ix–x.

10. Earnest R. Archer, "How to Make a Business Decision: An Analysis of Theory and Practice," *Management Review* 69 (February 1980): 55.

11. Henry Mintzberg, "Planning on the Left Side and Managing on the Right," *Harvard Business Review* 54 (July/August 1976): 55.

12. Mintzberg, Raisinghani, and Théorêt, "The Structure" p. 246.

13. Lawrence A. Gordon, Danny Miller, Henry Mintzberg, *Normative Models in Managerial Decision-Making* (New York: National Association of Accountants, 1975), p. 1.

14. For examples of decision trees, see Howard Raiffa, *Decision Analysis*; for decision tables, see Michael D. Resnick, *Choices: An Introduction to Decision Theory* (Minneapolis: Univ. of Minnesota Press, 1987); for decision flowcharts, see Gordon, Miller, Mintzberg, *Normative Models*.

15. Mintzberg, "Planning on the Left Side," p. 55.

16. Ibid., p. 55.

17. Mintzberg, Raisinghani, and Théorêt, "The Structure," pp. 263–266.

18. Arlyn J. Melcher, *Structure and Process of Organizations: A Systems Approach* (Englewood Cliffs, NJ: Prentice-Hall, 1976), p. 154.

19. Beatrice Kovacs, "Decision-Making in Collection Development: Medical School Libraries." (D. L. S. diss., Columbia University, 1983). This design was implemented in public, academic, and school libraries over a period of years.

20. Mintzberg, "Planning on the Left Side," p. 55.

21. Ibid.

22. Mintzberg, Raisinghani, and Théorêt, "The Structure," pp. 263–266.

23. Melcher, *Structure and Process*, p. 154.

PART II
CASE STUDIES

INTRODUCTION

Developing library collections involves continual decision making that is specific to the environment in which the collections are to be housed and used. General theories of decision making and specific suggestions as to how the theories are to be applied are helpful in generating an awareness of the processes involved. Unless these theories are examined in light of specific situations, however, they are often unclear to persons who do not have the educational background and training of the organizational theorist. Practical applications are difficult to determine without examples to clarify the theories. Therefore, selectors in a number of libraries were interviewed and their decision-making processes were identified.

The interviews were conducted in sets. Each set of interviews occurred in the same period of time in a particular type of library located in the same geographic region. The first set of interviews was conducted in special libraries, specifically in medical school libraries.[1]

The second set of interviews occurred in school media centers and was conducted by Bobbie M. Pell, who replicated the study design used previously. With the unexpected, yet reasonable, finding that the decision-making processes for selectors in school media centers are basically the same as for selectors in the medical school libraries, it was decided that the study would be replicated in public libraries[2] and in academic libraries.

In each set of interviews, four libraries were selected from the pool of available libraries. Care was taken to assure that the libraries had differing organizational structures, since the purpose of the research was to identify the mental processes of selectors' decision making. These mental processes might, or might not, be affected by the selector's place in the organization.

The geographic areas of service, or the types of clientele for which services were provided, might also impact the decision-making processes and were therefore indentified. Whenever possible, libraries of the same type (i.e., public libraries, academic libraries, etc.) were located in the same geographic region to eliminate the possibility of regional differences impacting the decision-making processes.

A second variable was eliminated by conducting the interviews of selectors in a type of library during the same period of time, so that influences such as legislative, historic, or regional occurrences would not impact some selectors without being relevant to others in the same type of library. The selectors in the school libraries were interviewed during the months of October and November, while they still had some funds to expend. Selectors in special, public, and academic libraries were interviewed during the months of February, March, and part of April, depending on the interviewees' schedules.

Since many people are unaware of their decision-making processes, it was determined that each selector would need to be interviewed more than once. The interviews were conducted weekly for six to eight weeks; the same eight open-ended questions were asked each week (see Appendix K). The selectors came to anticipate those questions and to note any occurrences during the intervening days that would be of relevance to the study. These responses were then codified according to the framework identified by Mintzberg[3] and the levels of discretion described by Melcher.[4]

To understand the decision making of the selectors interviewed, it is necessary to understand the nature of the libraries for which they worked. Therefore, descriptions of the libraries that participated in this research and the collection development programs within those libraries follow.

NOTES

1. Kovacs, "Decision-Making in Collection Development."
2. The research in public libraries was made possible through a grant from the Public Libraries Section of the North Carolina Library Association.
3. Mintzberg, "Planning on the Left Side," pp. 49–58.
4. Melcher, *Structure and Process*, p. 154.

4

Case Studies: Public Libraries

CITY "A" PUBLIC LIBRARY

Organization

Location and Size. City "A" Public Library is located in a small city. There is one branch, which serves a minority neighborhood. There is no room for expansion in the main library and the collection of print and media materials is overcrowded.

Organizational Structure. All departments report to the director and the assistant director (Figure 4.1). One-fourth of the 40 employees have professional degrees, the remainder are clerical or nonprofessional, and there are virtually no students hired by the library.

Physical Facility and Collection Size. The collection, housed in a 40,000 square foot facility, consists of almost 250,000 volumes, 11,000 paperbacks, and a variety of audiovisual materials including phonorecordings, art prints, microforms, 16mm films, filmstrips, and over 500 videocassettes.

Budget

For the year studied, the total budget for City "A" Public Library was $1.5 million, of which $200,000 was budgeted for purchase of ma-

Figure 4.1
City "A" Public Library Organizational Chart

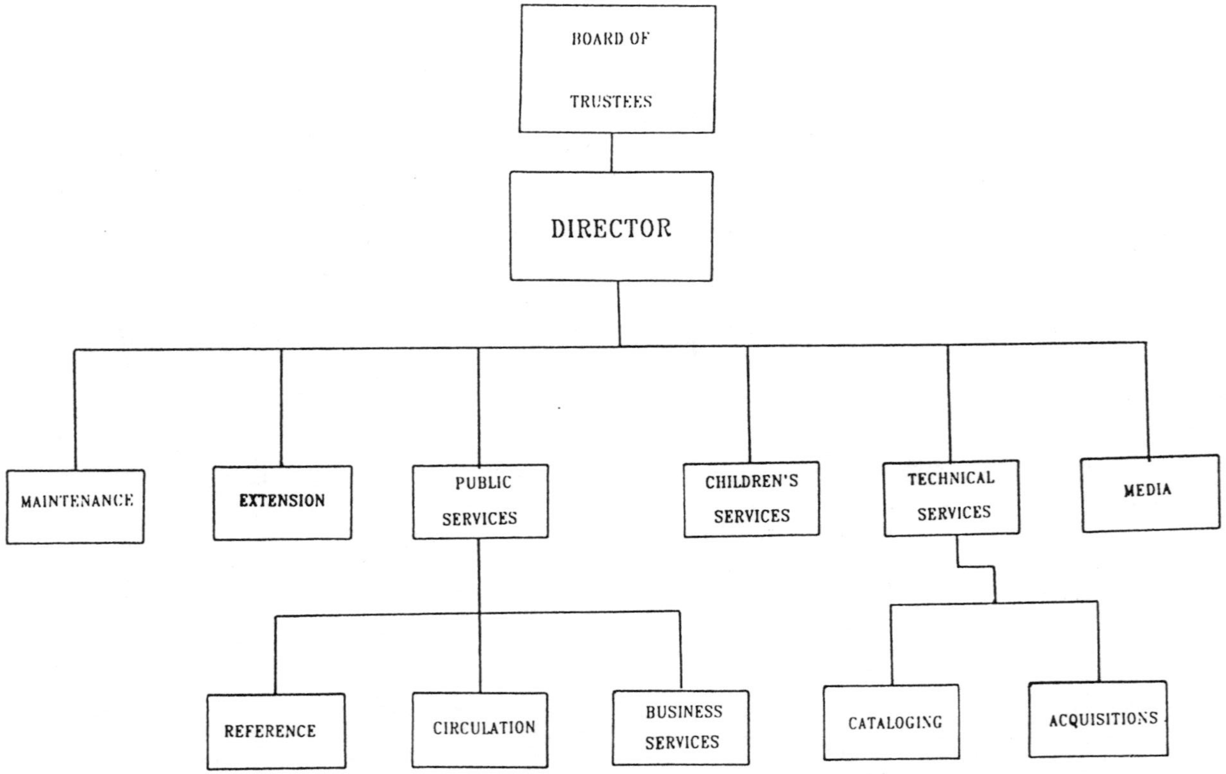

terials for the collections. Monies are received from local, state, and federal funding sources, as well as from small donations by individuals during the year.

The budget for the collections is allocated in several ways. Money is generally allocated by "activity," and then line by line. The exception to "activity" allocation is money set aside for periodical subscriptions, which are initially subtracted from the collection budget. The remaining funds' allotment is decided by the selectors, working with the administration of the library. Within the "activity" designations, lines are provided to purchase monographs, periodicals, serials, blanket orders, retrospective materials, audio and visual media, and special collections.

Once the budget is exhausted, titles for purchase are held until the release of funds in the next fiscal year. Most of the collection funds were expended by March, although the fiscal year ended June 30. Therefore, there were a number of titles held until the next fiscal year. Only orders for items that were needed immediately were processed and sent for purchase by the head of technical services.

Collection Development Program

There is a somewhat formal collection development program at the City "A" Public Library. There is a collection development policy (see Appendix A).

Selection Responsibility. All staff have the responsibility to select materials for the collections. One person, the head of technical services, is designated as responsible for checking the recommendations from the staff. Occasionally, the head of technical services identifies materials that might be considered questionable or sensitive, or might have contents that could be challenged by the patrons; he then sends them to the director of the library for final decision. The head of technical services is also designated the primary selector for local history materials.

Selection Procedures. Selectors forward recommendations for purchase to their department heads, who have the first opportunity to accept or reject the selections. Recommendations received from the public are also given to the appropriate department head for review. Approved recommendations are forwarded to the head of technical services. Pre-order searching is conducted in Technical Services; purchase recommendations are checked against the on-order file and the holdings file for the library. Duplicates are rejected; items that are not duplicates are searched to confirm the bibliographic data. Titles of items approved for purchase are sent to the appropriate vendor or other distribution source.

Study Participants. Four selectors agreed to participate in the study. They were the head of technical services, the head of adult services, the head of children's services, and a reference/technical services librarian.

The selectors identified a number of ways in which they became aware of titles appropriate for purchase for the collections. In order of frequency, they were:

1. listings of new books in reviewing sources
2. replacements for worn, damaged, or lost materials
3. patron requests for titles not already on order
4. new editions of titles in the collections
5. upcoming programs and support of the local school curriculum (responses from the head of children's services exclusively)

The selectors were asked if there were any examples of titles they had approved for order but were not actually purchased or added to their collection. The head of technical services remarked that during the study period there was one book he had recommended which, when received and examined, he felt was inappropriate for the collections because of the method of treatment of the topic. He submitted it for review by the director and it was not added to the collections.

The head of children's services had requested several titles that were duplications of items already in the children's collection. She was able to cite three examples of items ordered but not added to the children's collection:

1. a book purchased for children's reference which, upon examination, she felt "really belonged in the adult collection"
2. a book that was physically too small to be added to the collection
3. a book that she recommended for purchase, but then withdrew from the purchase process because after some thought she felt that although the reviews of the book were good, the title given to the book was likely to inhibit the book's use by the target age group and it would not be checked out

Several books recommended by the head of public services were not purchased because they were already out-of-stock or out-of-print. She also mentioned one book requested by a patron that was more appropriate for, and therefore added to, the children's collection.

The reference technical services librarian reconsidered several items before he sent them to his department head for purchase. These included an experimental novel that was unlikely to be read by the patrons of the library and a book that had a biased view toward a controversial organization and for which there was no opposing view available to provide balance in the collection.

Collection Evaluation. Evaluations of the collections at City "A" Public Library have never been conducted, although the director of the library felt that such evaluations should be done. When asked why none had been instituted, he responded that "it is labor intensive." Ten years prior to this research, a use study had been conducted, but the findings were considered no longer valid and had no impact on the current collection development program.

Collection Weeding and Deselection. There is no active weeding or deselection program at City "A" Public Library. Items discarded during the study period were books that were damaged or worn and books that were old and contained out-of-date information. A few of the worn books were re-ordered. The head of children's services discarded duplicates, as well as damaged books, because she had a space problem and needed to make room on the shelves for new books.

CITY "B" PUBLIC LIBRARY

Organization

Location and Size. Located in the same county as the City "A" Public Library, City "B" Public Library serves a moderate-sized city. There are six branches throughout the city, one small branch located in the county, a bookmobile, and two outreach programs.

Organizational Structure. Library operations are divided into three divisions: Main Library; Support Services; and Extension Services (Figure 4.2). The Main Library is responsible for circulation, reference, audiovisual, and children's departments in the Main Library. Support Services includes data processing, acquisitions, cataloging, processing, and building maintenance in the Main Library. Extension Services is responsible for the branches, the bookmobile, and the two outreach programs supported by the system. All divisions report to the director of the library; there is no associate director. Of the 70 full-time employees, 30 have their M.L.S. degrees and 40 are staff or clerical employees. In addition, there are approximately 10 student pages employed by the library during the year.

Physical Facility and Collection Size. The branches vary in size and collection content. The Main Library contains 215,000 volumes, plus 1,500 16mm films, 12,000 phonorecordings, and over 200 videotapes

Figure 4.2
City "B" Public Library Organizational Chart

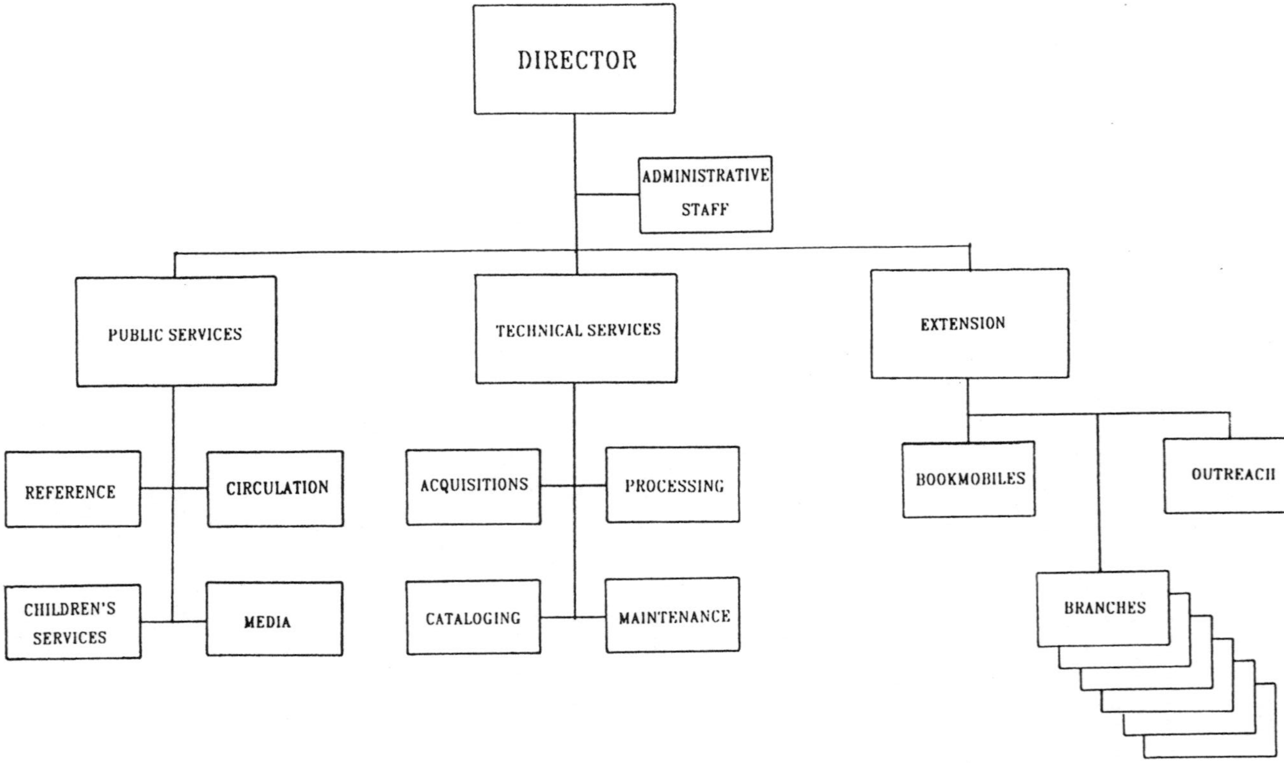

in the 75,000 square foot building. Recently, City "B" had purchased an adjacent building for use by the library, which would add 10,000 square feet for collections and services.

City "B" Public Library has pioneered the use of an integrated computer-based library system within the region. It was the first local library to have an automated on-line public access catalog and automated circulation. The original system was created in-house over five years prior to the study and was no longer adequate for the library. Therefore, a new system was being installed. For a period of time during the study there was no access to the data bases, including the on-line catalog, the borrower records, and the circulation records.

Budget

The budget for library operations was $3 million, with nearly $600,000 budgeted for the collections. Funds are received from local, state, regional, and federal sources. Some gift monies were donated by the Friends of the Library.

The collection budget is created through the use of a formula developed by the director of the library. This formula is based on a number of factors, most of which are identified through the statistics produced by the integrated library system. Unfortunately, the old system was so inadequate for the library that necessary statistics were not available, and allocations were estimated. The director of the library expects that statistics generated by the new system, once all current information is input, will provide an accurate picture of the collections and their use. Then the formulas for the budgets of various subject areas of the collections can be revised.

Funds are spent on monographs, periodicals, serials, audio and visual media, special collections, and rental books. Once all funds are expended, purchase recommendations are held until the following fiscal year that begins on July 1. Fund accounting was awkward during the changeover in computer systems, and the selectors were not sure how much money they had remaining in their allocations. Most of those selectors participating in the study indicated that they thought they were out of money by the end of March.

Collection Development Program

The collection development program at City "B" Public Library is in a period of change. A Collection Development Committee was appointed and is currently in the process of creating a collection development policy. The only existing policy concerning the collections is

a statement on materials appropriate for purchase for the nondeposi-
tory government documents collection (see Appendix B).

Selection Responsibility. All professional staff are responsible for
selecting materials for the collections. Each professional staff member
has an area of the collection assigned to him/her. Purchase recommendations are also accepted from the public and are forwarded for
consideration to the selector responsible for that area of the collections.

Selection Procedures. All purchase recommendations approved by
the designated selectors are sent to the head of technical services for
order. Pre-order searching is conducted by the Technical Services staff
and follows the same process as at City "A" Public Library. Unfortunately, again due to the changeover in computer systems, selectors
and Technical Services staff were unable to determine whether titles
requested were duplications of materials already held because the
catalog was not accessible. Records of material ordered prior to the
shutdown of the old system were unavailable as well. During several
months, there was the unfortunate but unavoidable possibility of purchasing duplicates. Purchase requests made during the shutdown period were recorded in paper files that could be checked.

Study Participants. Three selectors at the City "B" Public Library
agreed to participate in the study. They were the head of children's
services, government documents librarian, and local history librarian.

During the study period, the selectors became aware of titles for
purchase in several ways. Most frequently, selectors identified titles
for purchase through reading publications that list new books. Patron
requests were the second most frequent method of identifying materials for purchase. The head of children's services also listed new editions, replacements for worn books, and books to support upcoming
programs.

Only one title was rejected for purchase during the study period.
That title, recommended and then rejected by the government documents librarian, was a book about individual retirement accounts
published by the Internal Revenue Service prior to tax reforms en-
acted by Congress. He felt that it would not be helpful, and might
even mislead patrons using it, so he cancelled the order and will wait
for the new edition.

With the exception of some changes of mind by the selectors during
the study period, there were no other items rejected for purchase once
the recommendations were forwarded to Technical Services. It must
be noted, however, that there was the potential for inadvertent duplication of materials already held in the collections because the selec-

tors and Technical Service staff were unable to check the catalog for holdings.

Collection Evaluation. Evaluations and use studies of the collections were conducted continually through the use of the computer, with consequent revisions in the budget formulas for monetary allocations. It was expected that the new computer system would be of sufficient strength and size to permit even more sophisticated data gathering on the use of the collections by patrons, the subject strengths and weaknesses that the selectors need to address, and the overall growth and direction of the collections owned by the City "B" Public Library and its extension services.

Collection Weeding and Deselection. Without the input available from the computer, weeding and deselection were at a minimum. The head of children's services discarded a few books that were damaged or in poor condition. The government documents librarian discarded one outdated reference book and removed some older materials from the active collection to a less accessible stack area in the building. The local history librarian remarked that as the collection under his control is archival, he is not permitted to discard materials without the approval of the head of public services, and he rarely identified titles that might be appropriate for removal.

COUNTY "C" PUBLIC LIBRARY

Organization

Location and Size. Within 30 miles of both City "A" Public Library and City "B" Public Library is the County "C" Public Library. There is one moderate-sized city in the county, in which the Main Library is headquartered. There are eight branches, two bookmobiles, and several outreach services for the people of the county.

Organizational Structure. The director and the associate director oversee two divisions: Main Library Division and Extension Division (Figure 4.3). The head of the main library division is responsible for all services at the Main Library, including adult and children's services; there is no Technical Services Department in the system (all cataloging and processing of materials is done elsewhere). The head of extension division coordinates all branch, bookmobile, and outreach services. There is an almost even number of professional and nonprofessional staff: 40 with M.L.S. degrees and 45 staff and clerical employees. County "C" Public Library also hires approximately 30 student pages.

Physical Facility and Collection Size. There is 100,000 square feet

Figure 4.3
County "C" Public Library Organizational Chart

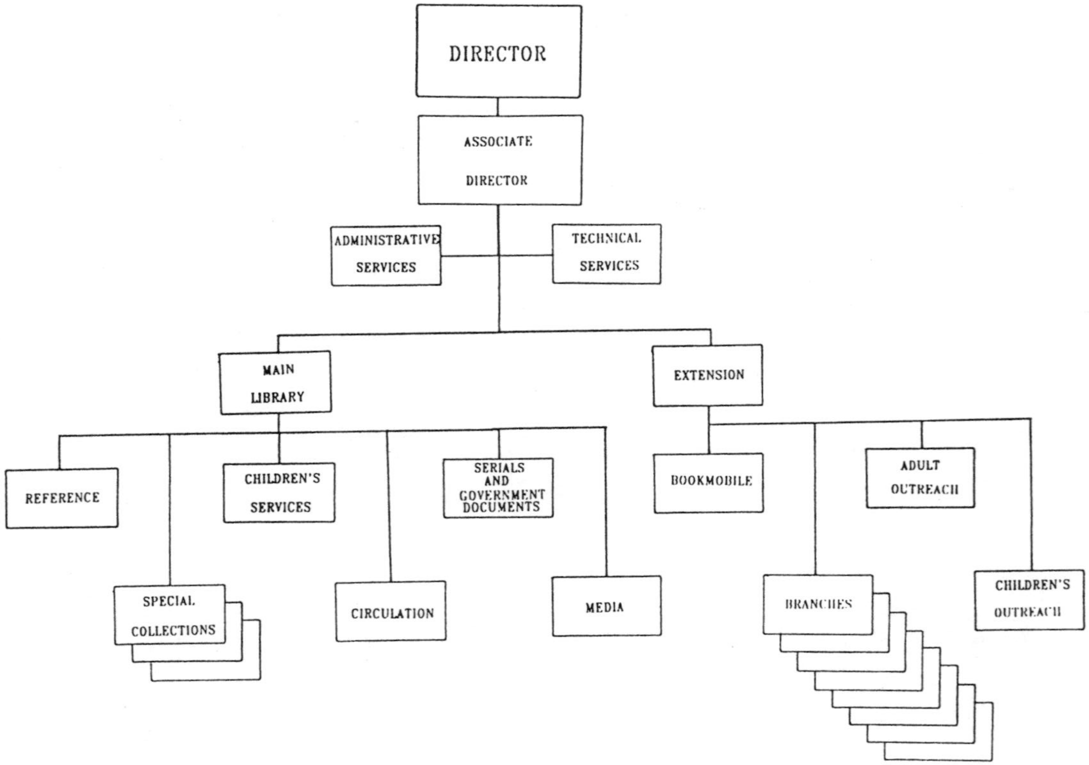

of space in the Main Library, which contains 175,000 volumes, 10,000 microforms, and a large number of audio and video formats. Total holdings for the system number 325,000 volumes. The Main Library facility, according to the director of the library, was designed for 20 years' growth and still has approximately 16 years' growth space left.

Budget

Funding was almost $4 million for the year studied, with money received from local, state, and federal sources, as well as gifts and some endowment funds. Of the total budget, $400,000 was allotted for collections.

The library has a line-item budget. The money is allocated into the following categories:

1. planned expenditures such as serials, standing orders, and encyclopedias
2. Main Library divisions such as adult services, children's services, management and technology, local history, and continuing education
3. Extension Services, including materials for the branches, bookmobiles, and outreach programs

The administration of the County "C" Public Library recommended that all selectors expend their allotted funds by April 1. Since this date fell within the study period, there was an opportunity to examine how the selectors dealt with an expected three-month period without the ability to purchase new materials, since the new fiscal year did not start until July 1.

Collection Development Program

County "C" Public Library has an informal collection development program that relies on the selectors' knowledge and user requests to identify materials for the collections. There is a selection policy (see Appendix C) approved by the Board of Trustees during the early 1970s that includes statements of policy on weeding the collections, gifts of materials, and duplication of titles.

Selection Responsibility. All professional staff have the responsibility to select materials for the collections. Requests from other staff and from the public are welcome also.

Selection Procedures. Recommendations from selectors, staff, and the public are examined by the heads of the relevant departments. Recommendations for purchase approved by the head of a department are sent to the administrative assistant, who prepares the orders and sends them to the supplier. As long as collection funds are available, materials are ordered. Once the budget is depleted, orders are held until the next fiscal year.

There is no department in this library system that has the responsibility for technical services, processing, acquisitions, or similar function. All materials purchased for the library system are sent to a central processing facility where they are cataloged and physically processed. Therefore, there is no pre-order searching conducted, nor is there an opportunity to batch multiple-copy orders for several departments. The administrative assistant's only duty is to prepare and send the orders to the center.

Study Participants. Three selectors agreed to participate in the study. They were the head of adult services, the head of children's services, and the head of management and technology department.

The selectors identified titles in a number of ways. In order of frequency, the methods were:

1. listings of new books in reviewing sources
2. patron requests for titles
3. replacements for worn, damaged, or lost materials
4. upcoming programs support
5. support of the local curriculum for children and adults
6. new editions of titles in the collections

Occasionally selectors changed their minds regarding potential purchases. Otherwise, the only materials requested, but not ordered, were materials identified as duplications of titles in the collections, or titles received on the rental plan.

Collection Evaluation. A committee, created by the County "C" Public Library, conducted an evaluation of the adult book collections held in all departments of the system during this study period. One part of the evaluation involved examination of the system's shelflist. The results of this evaluation included the identification of subject areas that needed upgrading, and the fact that a large percentage of the book collections was older than was considered appropriate for a public library (i.e., older than 5–10 years).

Another component of the evaluation was a use study. Through the use study, the committee determined that the collections were meeting the needs of the clientele. The committee concluded that while the needs were being met, the collections did need some updating and subsequently some departments received additional funding for purchase of materials in specified areas.

Collection Weeding and Deselection. Each department of the County "C" Public Library weeds any material as needed, without a coordinated systemwide weeding program. The Adult Services and Management and Technology Departments eliminated only old editions of reference books or books that were damaged. Children's Services discarded not only outdated or damaged books, but also "easy" books from an overcrowded section of shelves. The selectors could not say whether discarded materials were in other branches of the system or whether any branch copies should be eliminated also.

COUNTY "D" PUBLIC LIBRARY

Organization

Location and Size. The County "D" Public Library is actually a library system that serves two counties. There is one Main Library, three branches in each of the counties, and one bookmobile.

Organizational Structure. While there is one Board of Trustees for the County "D" Public Library comprised of members from both counties, there are two governing Library Boards as well as a dual structure in the organizational chart. (Figure 4.4).

The system employs 10 professional librarians and 25 staff or clerical employees. Aside from the director, there is a professional librarian charged with the responsibility for each of the county branch systems, head of adult services, head of children's services, and head of technical services.

Physical Facility and Collection Size. The Main Library has a cramped 15,000 square feet of space housing over 70,000 volumes. Throughout the two counties, the system has 150,000 volumes, and 24,000 audio or video items.

Budget

The budget for the two-county system was $1 million, with $175,000 budgeted for the collections. Funds were received from local, state, and federal funds, as well as from both county governments, endowments, and grants from other sources.

Budgets for collections are determined by a combination of line-item and formula allocations. Periodicals, serials, rental books, microforms for the computer-output catalog and blanket orders for large-print materials are line items in the budget. Remaining funds are allocated according to a formula that determines usage of the collec-

Figure 4.4
County "D" Public Library Organizational Chart

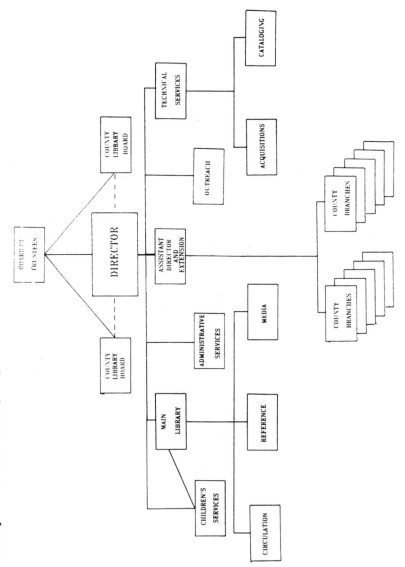

tions combined with the door count of the facility. Other materials purchased include monographs, retrospective materials, audio and visual media, and pamphlets and paperbacks. Some federal funds are designated for microcomputer software and videotapes, which cannot be purchased with regular budget money.

It is interesting to note that while the three preceding public libraries expended their budgets during the study period, the County "D" Public Library still had funds available that needed to be spent and the selectors had to identify additional items to order before the fiscal year ended on June 30.

Collection Development Program

This two-county system has the most formal collection development program of the four participating libraries. There is a collection development policy that was revised in 1984 and approved by the Board of Trustees (see Appendix D), with a planned revision in 1989.

Selection Responsibility. There is a Collection Development Committee (CDC), comprised of the director of the library, head of adult services, head of children's services, head of technical services, and both of the county librarians. Primary selection responsibility rests with this committee; recommendations are also accepted from the public.

Selection Procedures. The CDC meets weekly and selects materials for the system's libraries using the following process:

1. Selection tools, such as review journals and vendor catalogs, are received by the departments of the system;
2. Each department routes its copy of the selection tool to staff for comments and suggestions for purchase;
3. Comments, suggestions, and recommendations for purchase from staff are brought to the meetings of the CDC;
4. Patron requests are given to the head of technical services for ordering for the appropriate department or branch;
5. Selection sources are then examined, titles to be ordered are named by the CDC members, and the number of copies for all departments are identified;
6. ISBN numbers are entered into the BetaPhone℠ for transmission after the conclusion of the meeting.

During each meeting, one member checks the on-order file to determine whether the title was already ordered. Each week a specific selection source or type of material is identified for ordering, such as a particular issue of *Library Journal* or *School Library Journal*, paperback books, or videotapes.

Study Participants. As a result of the structure of the collection development process at the County "D" Public Library, individual participants were not identified for the purpose of the study. Instead, the CDC invited the researcher to attend the weekly meetings, during which much of the relevant information was gathered. Committee members agreed to complete a short questionnaire to gather data not appropriate to the discussions during the meetings but which would contain information parallel to data collected during the interviews with selectors at the other libraries.

Titles were ordered as a result of listings of new books in reviewing sources and patron requests during each week of the study period. New editions of currently held material, replacements for worn or missing books, and titles to support upcoming programs were the other methods by which materials were identified for order. During the study period, there were no examples of materials ordered by the CDC that were then not purchased.

Collection Evaluation. Evaluations of the collections and patron use studies are conducted regularly by the staff of all components of the system. These studies affect the formula for allocation of the budget and target subject areas needing attention in the collections.

Collection Weeding and Deselection. A few juvenile fiction titles were discarded during the study period. In addition, some worn books were weeded and not re-ordered for the adult collections.

SUMMARY

Located in the same geographic region, the four public libraries were very different in their organization, budget, and collection development programs. One library had a formal program with a committee; three libraries had all professional librarians responsible for selections but with varying levels of discretion and supervision. Three of the four libraries had a written collection development policy, and the fourth library was in the process of developing such a policy.

5

Case Studies: School Libraries

Bobbie M. Pell

SCHOOL "A" LIBRARY

Organization

Location and Size. School "A" Library serves a city public school of over 350 students in grades three through five.

Organizational Structure. There is one librarian at the School "A" Library. She has no support staff but has fourteen students whom she trains as volunteer helpers (Figure 5.1).

Physical Facility and Size. This library is housed in a room that measures almost 4,500 square feet, with no room for expansion. The shelves line the room and there are no stack areas. The facility includes study carrels, interest centers, and reading areas. The total number of items is almost 5,000, of which 1,500 are audio and visual media.

Budget

For the year studied, the budget for School "A" Library included $1,500 for collections, which is approximately 90 percent of the total

Figure 5.1
School "A" Organizational Chart

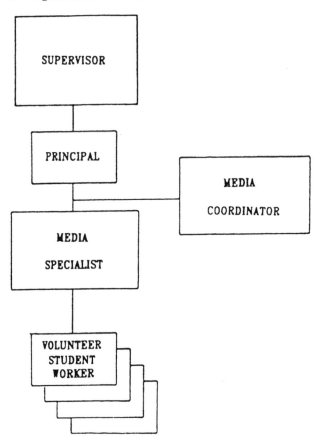

library budget, excluding the librarian's salary. The funds are received from federal, state, and local sources, as well as from gifts, fund raising, and parent-teacher organization donations. Because this school had undergone several grade shifts in the past few years, all instructional money (except for paper and supplies) is designated for instructional materials.

The collection money is allocated to School "A" Library in a lump-sum budget. The librarian has control over the way in which the money is spent, although she allocates funds to certain areas of need in the library depending on her annual assessment of the collection. This assessment, made with the help of the Media Advisory Committee, identifies areas of the collections that need updating or replacement.

All orders must be placed by mid-October, requiring the librarian to prioritize needed materials early in the school year.

Collection Development Program

All city public schools must follow the city's Board of Education policy, "Selection of Instructional Materials" (see Appendix E). In addition, there were policies for weeding and the receipt of gift materials (see Appendix G).

Selection Responsibility. According to the Board of Education Policy, the responsibility for evaluation of instructional materials is shared "jointly by members of the staff, members of the Media Advisory Committee and the media specialist (librarian)" (see Appendix E). The librarian is responsible for selecting materials for the library, but items purchased with school funds must be approved by the Media Advisory Committee and by the principal of the school. Patron requests for materials are welcome.

Selection Procedures. The librarian relied heavily on the standard selection and reviewing tools to identify materials that would be of value to the collection. Selections were checked against the shelflist to avoid duplication. Patron requests were checked against the shelflist, current reviews were examined, and possible purchases were then judged for price and relevancy to the collection and the curriculum. Orders for materials were then forwarded to the system-wide media supervisor.

Study Participants. The librarian at School "A" Library agreed to participate in the study. She identified a number of ways in which she became aware of material that would be appropriate for the collection. The standard selection tools were utilized most often because of the quality, reviews, and publishing information. Specialty journals were used to locate specific curriculum-related materials. General subject area reviews were found in the state advisory lists and other journals.

All titles originally ordered were purchased, but the media supervisor retained the right to decline any orders that she felt were unsuitable. There were no orders denied during the period of this study.

Collection Evaluation. With each grade shift in this school, the collection was evaluated to identify what materials would be needed to support the new curriculum. Analytical evaluations were conducted throughout the year in order to prioritize purchase orders according to recognized needs. In addition, an annual year-end inventory was done in accordance with state regulations. This inventory was to identify quantitative, not qualitative, information about the collection.

Collection Weeding and Deselection. With each grade shift, material inappropriate to the new curriculum was identified during the evaluation of the collection and removed to another school. Those materials that proved to be outdated or damaged were eliminated from the collection. If information contained in the damaged books was necessary to maintain a well-balanced collection, the books were replaced.

SCHOOL "B" LIBRARY

Organization

Location and Size. The second city public school library is in School "B." The school has a student population of 420 from kindergarten through second grade.

Organizational Structure. The librarian in charge of this library has no staff or, due to the young age of the students, any student volunteers. She does have, however, five parent volunteers to help with shelving, circulation, and routine clerical duties (Figure 5.2).

Physical Facility and Size. The room in which the library is located contains 2,000 square feet. There are four stack ranges. The collection numbers 6,500 volumes of print material and 4,000 audio or visual media, for a total of 10,500 items.

Budget

The collection budget for School "B" Library totaled almost $5,000. As with School "A" Library, the funds are received from federal, state, and local sources, as well as from gifts, fund raising, and parent-teacher organization donations.

The money is allocated to the library in a lump sum, and the library follows the same protocols and procedures as School "A" Library.

Collection Development Program

Again, as part of the city public school system, School "B" Library must follow the city's Board of Education policy, "Selection of Instructional Materials" (see Appendix E). School "B" Library also has policies for weeding and for receipt of gift materials (see Appendix G).

Selection Responsibility. Once again, the librarian is responsible for selecting materials. However, purchases are not made until approval

Figure 5.2
School "B" Organizational Chart

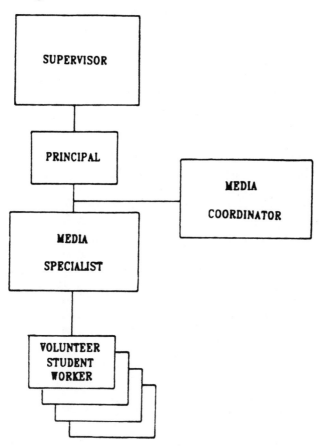

has been given by the Media Advisory Committee and by the principal of the school. Recommendations by patrons are screened by the librarian, the Media Advisory Committee, and the principal for relevancy and appropriateness in the maintenance of a well-balanced collection. During the screening process, the librarian checks outstanding orders and the current shelflist to avoid duplications. The librarian also analyzes similar materials already in the collection to see if additional materials on that topic are of value.

Selection Procedures. Once the screened requests have been approved, they are added to the list of new materials that have been selected according to collection needs. These materials are then prioritized by the librarian and ordered when funds are available. The orders are sent for review to the media supervisor for the school system. The media supervisor reserves the right to deny any orders that she feels are unsuitable for that collection.

Study Participants. The librarian at School "B" Library agreed to participate in the study. She identified a number of ways in which she became aware of material that would be appropriate for the collection. She most often consulted standard selection sources and review sections of professional journals. Subject specialty reviews such as those found in the state advisory lists also proved to be very helpful in maintaining a balanced collection closely related to the curriculum.

Titles that were originally ordered by the librarian at School "B" were purchased with no orders denied. The media supervisor retained the final approval of the purchases.

Collection Evaluation. An annual evaluation is conducted at School "B" in the form of an inventory at the close of each year in accordance with requirements of the city public school policy (see Appendix E). Informal evaluations are conducted throughout the year in conjunction with material selection to assess the needs of the collection.

Collection Weeding and Deselection. Weeding the collection is an on-going process throughout the school year. Those materials eliminated from the collection were either damaged, worn out, or outdated. Some damaged books were re-ordered if important to the collection.

SCHOOL "C" LIBRARY

Organization

Location and Size. Within this geographic region, the city that is served by School "A" and School "B" has its own school system. It is not affiliated with the county school system, for which there is another governing board. School "C" is part of the county system. This county school has a student population of 500 from kindergarten through fifth grade.

Organizational Structure. There is one librarian in charge of School "C" Library. She has one part-time aide who helps with clerical duties, class instruction, and book selection. In addition, she has two parent volunteers and 24 students workers (Figure 5.3).

Physical Facility and Size. School "C" Library is located in a room that measures almost 3,000 square feet. There are three stack ranges that hold 12,500 volumes of print materials and 1,500 audio and visual media items.

Figure 5.3
School "C" Organizational Chart

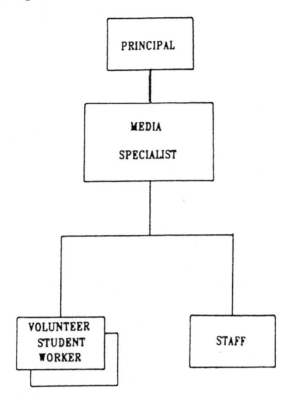

Budget

There is a $3,000 budget for collections at School "C" Library. This budget includes funds from federal, state, local, and fund-raising sources, as well as from gifts and parent-teacher organization donations.

School "C" Library receives its collection money in a lump sum, as do the city school libraries. Within this allotment, the media supervisor might suggest line-item percentages to be spent on specific types of materials (i.e., books, audiovisuals, equipment). The librarian is responsible for assessing overall needs of the collection, prioritizing those needs, and then purchasing items as the funds allow. Needs identified during the previous year influence the allocations for specific collection areas, along with replacements and material needed to update the collection.

Collection Development Program

During the time of this study, the county system was in the process of developing selection policies that would address the area-specific needs and priorities. A board of media specialists, in collaboration with media administrators, hoped to develop a balanced media manual in accordance with state standards and any relevant guidelines developed by the Southern Association of Colleges and Schools. During this interim period, the system adheres solely to the policies developed by the state's Department of Education in 1986 (see Appendix F).

Selection Responsibility. As in the city school media centers, the librarian and the Media Advisory Committee are responsible for material selection. The faculty is encouraged to make requests specific to their grade-level curriculum needs. Student requests are taken into consideration.

Selection Procedures. In selecting materials, the librarian compares faculty requests with the outstanding order file and with similar materials already in the collection. She then advises the Media Advisory Committee of her analysis. The librarian and the Media Advisory Committee prioritize all requests in light of curriculum needs, with an effort to maintain a balanced collection. Purchases are made in accordance with budget allowances.

Study Participants. The librarian at School "C" Library agreed to participate in this study. She identified several ways in which she became aware of material that would be appropriate for the collection. In order of frequency, they were the standard selection sources and state advisory lists for the highest quality reviews. Professional journals were used to locate recommended current titles for specific curriculum areas. Vendor catalogs are used in the county school more frequently than in the city schools, due to the fact that the county system does not have centralized processing and schools work directly with jobbers and vendors. Orders are often given directly to the sales people, bypassing the media supervisor. Titles, therefore, were not rejected for purchase.

Collection Evaluation. As in the city public school libraries, an inventory is done annually to comply with state and local mandates. The librarian also conducts informal evaluations throughout the year, to alert her to areas in the collection that need to be expanded or updated.

Collection Weeding and Deselection. Weeding in this library was done throughout the year to eliminate materials that were outdated, damaged, or worn out. Some of these materials were either re-ordered or rebound, depending on their current value and need in the collection.

Figure 5.4
School "D" Organizational Chart

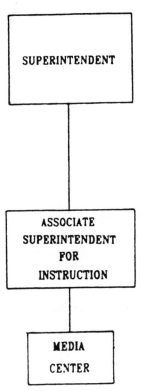

SCHOOL "D" LIBRARY

Organization

Location and Size. The fourth media center for this study is located in School "D", a private school supported primarily by a religious denomination. It is located in the same geographic region as the three previous schools. There are over 300 students, from kindergarten through eighth grade.

Organizational Structure. In addition to the librarian, there are two part-time clerical helpers and three parent volunteers. Student volunteers were available during their free time, but not on a regular basis (Figure 5.4).

Physical Facility and Size. The 2,500 square feet of space in this library includes five stack ranges and wall units. The collection contains almost 6,000 volumes of print materials and 500 audio and visual materials.

Budget

School "D" Library has the smallest budget of the four participating libraries. The collection budget for the period studied was $700. Of the four libraries studied, this was the only library that received a budget supplement during the last five years. The local and federal monies are given directly to the librarian, whereas money is indirectly issued through the Central Office Administration in the other three schools. Gifts and fund-raisers, along with parent-teacher organization donations, proved necessary because of the lack of state funds.

The library's budget is allocated according to a line-item budget, with specific stipulations as to how the money may be spent (i.e., specific percentages for books, reference materials, audiovisual materials, or equipment). In most cases, these specified funds are not transferable to other categories. The librarian has control over how the money should be spent and bases her decisions on past collection decisions, annual collection evaluations, replacement needs, and information that needs to be updated.

Collection Development Program

The collection development policy utilized in this library affirms the "Library Bill of Rights," "School Library Bill of Rights," and the "Student's Right To Read." Since this school is not governed by the state, the state's basic curriculum is not followed, but the collection development policy closely parallels the requirements of the state policy (see Appendix H).

Selection Responsibility. Due to the absence of a Media Advisory Committee and media supervisor, the librarian is solely responsible for materials selection. The principal reviews the orders and may deny any selections that appear inappropriate for the collections. This veto power had not been exercised during this librarian's eight years of service. The librarian relies heavily on teacher input and encourages student and parent input also. When questioned about the absence of a Media Advisory Committee, the librarian expressed her desire for one and hoped to create one soon in order to maintain a balanced collection.

Study Participants. The librarian at School "D" agreed to be a participant in this study. As in School "C," this librarian does not have access to centralized processing, so she deals directly with jobbers and vendors. There were several standard selection tools that she uses in making her materials selections. She also scans publisher's advertisements and catalogs, along with vendor lists and catalogs.

Collection Evaluation. The collection is formally evaluated during a year-end inventory. There are also informal evaluations throughout the year. Areas identified with specific needs are noted and taken into consideration for acquisition in the upcoming year.

Collection Weeding and Deselection. Weeding and deselection are conducted in accordance with the weeding policy for this school library (see Appendix H). Specific guidelines are given for each Dewey Decimal Classification area, including length of shelf time and currency of material. Fiction titles are discarded if they are damaged, worn, or contain inaccurate or inappropriate material, are replaceable with higher quality of literature or format, or are "excess baggage"—those books that do not circulate more than twice in three years. With the wide grade range and limited space, weeding is conducted critically and continually.

SUMMARY

Four elementary school libraries were similar in their collection development plans and policies yet varied in organization, budgets, and selection responsibilities. The two city public school libraries were almost identical due to their close tie to the Central Office and its policies. All four libraries had written collection development policies, and the librarians played a major role in the materials selection decisions.

6

Case Studies: Academic Libraries

COLLEGE "A" LIBRARY

Organization

Location and Size. College "A" Library serves a moderate-sized private college in a geographic area rich in resources for academic institutions. The city in which College "A" is located has four other college or university libraries and the metropolitan area includes at least five additional colleges or universities. The student population averages 1,230 undergraduates.

Organizational Structure. All departments report to the director of the library (Figure 6.1). At the time of the study, there was no associate director, although there were plans to fill the position in the future. Of the 15 library employees, 8 are professional librarians and the rest are staff or clerical workers. In addition, each year the library employs an average of 25 students as pages.

Physical Facility and Collection Size. The collections consist of over 215,000 items, with 20,000 audio and visual items. The library building, located in the heart of the campus, is four floors high with a total of 40,000 square feet. Stack and office space are so crowded that the

Figure 6.1
College "A" Library Organizational Chart

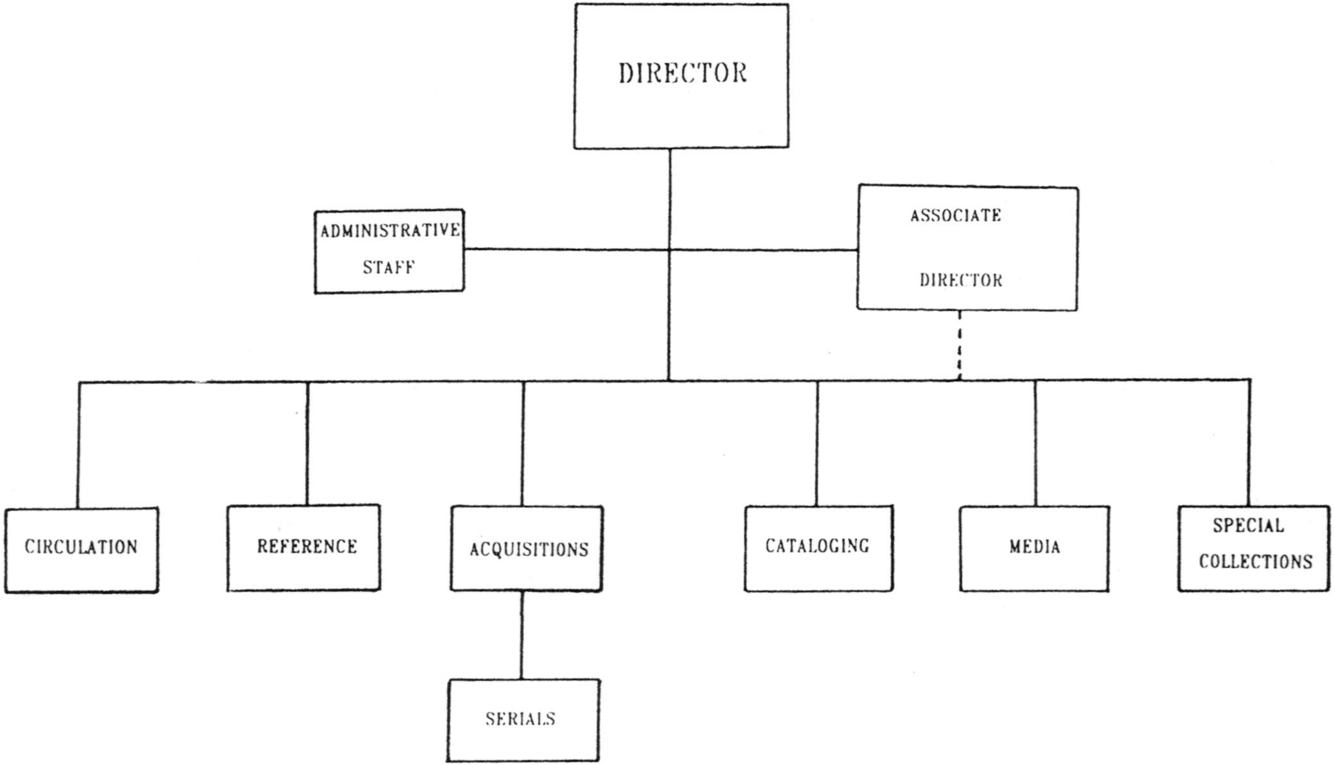

administration approved a new addition to the building, and construction was scheduled to begin almost immediately.

Budget

The budget for College "A" Library is a combination of funds from endowments, tuition, fund raising, and gifts, which totalled $500,000 during the study period. Of this, $150,000 was designated for purchase of materials for the collections.

Allocations for the collections are designated in a line-item budget. The allotments per line are determined by the director, selected members of the library staff, and/or the Faculty Library Committees. Funds are spent for monographs, periodicals, serials, and audio and visual media. There are also allocations for retrospective collecting and special collections. Once all funds are expended, recommendations for purchase are held until the next fiscal year.

Collection Development Program

College "A" Library is in the process of re-evaluating its collection development program. A collection development policy had been created 15 years ago, but it is no longer appropriate for the library. A Collection Development Committee has been appointed, and among the charges of the committee is the revision of the collection development policy. At present there are no written policies for weeding or for receipt of gift materials.

Selection Responsibility. All professional staff have the responsibility for the selection of materials for the collections. Purchase recommendations are accepted from students, alumni, and (according to the director of the library) "almost anybody."

Selection Procedures. Recommendations for purchase from library and college academic departments are sent directly to the Acquisitions Department for purchase. Recommendations for purchase from others are sent to the director of the library for review; approved items are sent to the Acquisitions Department also.

Study Participants. Three selectors agreed to participate in this study. They were the director of the library, the head of reference, and the head of acquisitions.

During the weekly interviews, the selectors identified the following ways in which they learned of titles to be purchased:

1. listings of new books in reviewing sources
2. patron requests for titles not already on order

3. materials appearing on specialized bibliographies

4. replacements for worn, damaged, or lost materials

5. new editions of titles in the collections

6. material to support upcoming programs in the college

All three selectors identified instances in which titles they had requested for purchase had been rejected. The primary reason for the rejection was duplication: the library either owned the item or had previously placed an order for it.

Collection Evaluation. The newly formed Collection Development Committee is in the process of evaluating the collection development program. A questionnaire was distributed to users to determine user satisfaction, but the results were not available during the study period.

Collection evaluation is considered an on-going process at the College "A" Library. Each "best" list is carefully checked against the library's catalog to identify potential additions to the collections. Circulation statistics are continually monitored, and fund allocations for subject departments within the college are sometimes based upon the number of circulations in the subject disciplines of the department.

Collection Weeding and Deselection. The director of the library did not identify any materials appropriate for withdrawal during the study period. The head of acquisitions deselected only gift materials that had been accepted in bulk shipments. Only the head of reference identified material already in the collections that was to be removed from the holdings. She spent several weeks identifying short, out-of-scope runs of periodicals to discard, as well as short runs of periodicals that could not be accessed through any of the indexing and abstracting sources held in the College "A" Library reference collection. She also discarded a few outdated or superseded titles in the collections.

COLLEGE "B" LIBRARY

Organization

Location and Size. The smallest of the four academic libraries included in the study is the College "B" Library. College "B" is a small private school, with slightly over 70 students, which is supported by, and supports, a Protestant denomination.

Organizational Structure. Of the one full and two part-time employees of the library, two have Master of Library Science degrees and one is a clerical employee. The director of the library reports directly

Figure 6.2
College "B" Library Organizational Chart

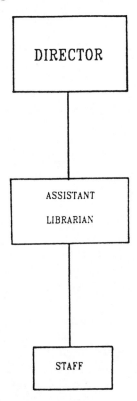

to the president of the college and has no advisory committee (Figure 6.2). Because the college is so small, however, the director of the library has a great deal of input from, and contact with, all the faculty, staff, and students of the college.

Physical Facility and Collection Size. The library has 3,000 square feet of space on one floor, which houses the 30,000 item collection. The collection includes almost 1,200 audio and visual items. There are plans for expansion of the library's space once additional buildings are built by the college. The new buildings are needed for classroom space, as the enrollment of the college has been increasing.

Budget

Tuition, gifts, some fund raising, and occasional book sales are the sources for funds for the library's budget. The total budget for the College "B" Library was $30,000 for the period studied, with $7,000 budgeted for the collections. For three of the five years prior to the study, the budget for the library was frozen so that the director of the library was unable to expend money as planned.

The budget for collections is determined by a program and performance budgeting system. The core list of periodicals is budgeted separately. Monograph allocations are developed by a combination of a formula for tuition fees and a percentage of the overall institution funds; media allocations are a percentage of the library budget. Retrospective and special collections materials are funded from outside sources, such as gift monies. There are no approval plans or blanket orders; serials are purchased from book funds. Once all funds are expended, or are frozen by the administration, purchase orders are held until the next fiscal year.

Collection Development Program

The College "B" Library is in the process of developing a formal collection development program. There is a collection development policy (see Appendix I), that was written by the director of the library one year prior to this study, and evaluation and revision of the policy is planned for every two to three years.

Significant changes in the collection development program over the previous years included the introduction of planned development for the collections, with a concern to continue development of an excellent collection. In the past, the collection had grown haphazardly through occasional purchases and the receipt of gift materials that were automatically added to the library.

Selection Responsibility. The director of the library is the selector for the library collections. Recommendations are welcome from faculty, staff, students, and alumni of the college.

Selection Procedures. The director determines what titles to order for the College "B" Library and sends the orders to the appropriate suppliers.

Study Participants. The director of the library agreed to participate in this study. During the weekly interviews, she identified the following ways in which she learned of titles to purchase (in order of frequency):

1. listings of new books in reviewing sources

2. vendor and publisher listings of new titles

3. patron requests for titles not already on order

4. material appearing in specialized bibliographies

During one week of the study period, the director identified some titles that she had originally selected but then did not order because she changed her mind.

Collection Evaluation. There was a recent evaluation of the reference collection of the College "B" Library, conducted by the director. Weaknesses were identified and a plan for addressing the weaknesses was developed. Additionally, a user study was conducted to identify weaknesses in the general collection.

Collection Weeding and Deselection. During each week of the study, the director identified items discarded from the collections. Most of the discards were duplicates or books that were out-of-date or out-of-scope for the collections. Some materials also discarded by the director were "by off the wall [by reputation] authors" or were books that had "trashy" coverage of the subject. As the director said, "I don't mess around. If a book is out of date, doesn't match the catalog record, and is irrelevant to this collection, I throw it out."

UNIVERSITY "C" LIBRARY

Organization

Location and Size. Part of the state university system, University "C" is a land-grant institution serving minority students. There is a historical specialization in agriculture and technology. The library is the primary library for this university unit, serving a population of almost 6,000 undergraduate and graduate students. There is also a small branch subject collection located in a department.

Organizational Structure. There are basically three divisions in the University "C" Library: Administrative Services, Public Services, and Technical Services (Figure 6.3). Employees of the library include 16 professional librarians with M.L.S. degrees, over 24 staff and clerical personnel, and approximately 51 student pages.

Physical Facility and Collection Size. The University "C" Library is located in a five-floor building, with approximately 81,000 square feet of space. Within this building, which is old and inadequate to provide the environmental and space requirements needed, are housed collections that number 650,000 volumes of print materials and over 16,000 audio and visual items. A new building is planned for the near future, but funding has not yet been approved.

Budget

Funding for the University "C" Library is received from federal, state, foundation, and endowment sources, and from gifts given to the

Figure 6.3
University "C" Library Organizational Chart

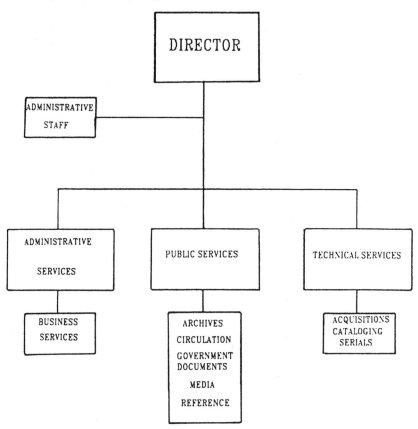

library during the year. Of the total $2 million budget for the year studied, $600,000 was budgeted for the collections. Occasionally there have been budget supplements to develop collections in disciplines for which new degree programs were approved.

The library receives funds in a lump sum, with an amount identified for the collections. This sum for collections is then allocated to collection areas by the use of a formula for various categories and subjects. Money is spent for monographs, periodicals, serials, approval plans, audio and visual media, and special collections. Once all available funds are expended, recommended titles are put into a desiderative file for order in the new fiscal year.

Collection Development Program

There is a somewhat formal collection development program at the University "C" Library. This program is based on the knowledge of the bibliographers and the requests of users to identify materials for the collections. There is a collection development policy that was written in the late 1970s that is currently under revision and was unavailable to the researcher. The policy includes statements of policy on weeding the collections, gifts of materials, and duplication of titles.

Selection Responsibility. Selection of materials for the collections is the responsibility of the subject bibliographers in the library and of the university faculty. Recommendations are accepted from students and alumni.

Selection Procedures. Recommendations from the subject bibliographers, students, alumni, faculty, and staff are forwarded to the head of technical services. He has primary authorization for the purchase of materials for the collections and forwards approved purchase requests to the Purchasing Department. The head of technical services generally approves recommendations for purchase as long as funds remain in the budget.

Study Participants. The head of technical services volunteered to participate in this study. Major sources used by him to identify materials for purchase were:

1. faculty requests for titles not already on order
2. bibliographer requests for titles not already on order
3. replacements for worn, damaged, or lost materials
4. vendor and publisher listings of new titles

One item, originally selected by the head of technical services, but which he later rejected for purchase, was an expensive indexing service. This indexing service was available at a nearby library that participates in a resource-sharing agreement with the University "C" Library. Otherwise, while he commented that he occasionally changes his mind regarding potential purchases, there were no examples of this occurring during the study.

Collection Evaluation. Evaluations of parts of the collections, and any use studies of materials in particular disciplines, are conducted only when accreditation teams require them. The results of the evaluations include the identification of subject areas that need upgrading, and the library follows the recommendations of the accrediting teams.

Collection Weeding and Deselection. There is no coordinated weeding program at the University "C" Library. During the study period,
the only materials discarded were old editions of reference books and
some books that were damaged.

UNIVERSITY "D" LIBRARY

Organization

Location and Size. University "D" is also part of the state university system, serving a large campus population with a graduate and
undergraduate body of over 10,000 students. There are several schools
and colleges, and post-graduate programs offering master's and doc-
torate degrees in a number of disciplines. The library serves all programs and departments of the university. There are small libraries
in two academic units on campus, but those collections are developed
and maintained independently of the library.

Organizational Structure. All departments of the library report to
the associate director and the director of the library (Figure 6.4). Of
the almost 90 employees of the library, one fourth are professional
librarians. The remainder are staff or clerical employees and student
workers. Statistics list over 20 full time equivalent student workers
(student workers whose hours worked, combined, equal 20 full-time
employees), but this figure represents over 200 individuals. Two committees that have advisory responsibilities to the director are the Faculty Library Committee and the Friends of the Library.

Physical Facility and Collection Size. The main library is located in
a building, expanded over a number of years, to provide a facility of
over 220,000 square feet in a varying number of floors. There is room
for expansion, but it is considered inadequate for the near future. A
new addition to the existing facility is planned within the next few
years. The collection consists of over 1 million volumes, with 19,000
audio and visual materials.

Budget

State, federal, tuition, grant, and revenue-account funds comprise
the budget of University "D" Library, with a number of gifts or fund-
raising by the Friends of the Library being donated each year. Of the
$7 million budgeted during the study year, approximately $1 million
was budgeted for the collections.

Funds are allocated by the line-item budget mandated by the state.
Allocations for subject areas are developed by formula based upon the
amount of funds specified by the state for monographs and print ma-

Figure 6.4
University "D" Library Organizational Chart

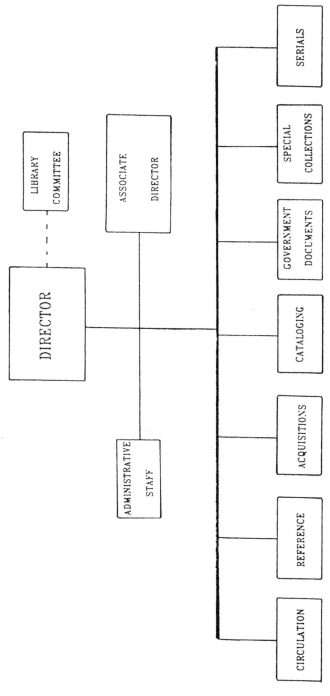

terials. Material purchased include monographs, periodicals, serials, blanket orders, retrospective materials, special collections, and phonograph records. Other media are generally not purchased, with the exception of an occasional piece of artwork for students to borrow to decorate their dorm rooms. No films, videotapes, cassette recordings, microcomputer software, or similar audiovisual material are purchased. Once all funds are expended, orders are held until the following fiscal year.

Collection Development Program

There is no formal collection development program at the University "D" Library. Some collection development policy or procedure statements were developed by some of the academic departments of the university, but there is no general policy for the development of the library's collection.

The Collection Development Committee, advisory to the director, is composed of several library faculty. In addition, there is a Library Committee that consists of members of the university faculty appointed by the university. There is no individual responsible for collection development in the library; rather, responsibility for parts of collection development are allocated to individuals on the staff.

Selection Responsibility. All staff have the opportunity to select materials for the collections. Purchase recommendations are accepted from students, alumni, and other interested individuals. In addition, there is a rather formal process by which academic departments forward purchase recommendations to a library representative in their school or college. This library representative is responsible for verifying the information about the item and assuring that it is not already held in the library, as well as for keeping track of the expenditure of the allotments for the disciplines.

Selection Procedures. Each selector's recommendations and academic department requests are forwarded to the Acquisitions Department, where the information is searched, verified, and applied against the budget. Orders for materials not already owned are sent to vendors.

Study Participants. Two selectors participated in the study. They were the head of reference and the head of acquisitions. During the weekly interviews, they identified the following ways in which they learned of titles to be purchased:

1. listings of new books in reviewing sources

2. patron requests for titles not already on order

3. material to support the curriculum

4. material to support upcoming programs in the university

5. new editions of titles in the collections

During the study period, there were a few examples of items ordered by one of the selectors but then rejected for purchase. The head of reference mentioned during the first week that one item ordered was not available because the publisher decided not to publish it; one book was rejected after arrival because of the poor quality of the content; and a book received on blanket order was rejected as being inappropriate in subject. During the third week, two books arriving on blanket order were rejected as out-of-scope. A microfilm collection purchased on the basis of advertisements was deemed inappropriate for the library and returned during the fourth week. In the fifth week, an order for a book copyrighted three years earlier was cancelled because the book had not yet been published; in the last week of the study, duplicates and spinoffs of materials in the collections were rejected for purchase. No items approved for purchase by the head of acquisitions were rejected for purchase.

Collection Evaluation. There have been several evaluations of the collections during the past few years, including a major self-study mandated by the university administration, and reports for various accrediting bodies. Use studies are conducted regularly by the head of circulation; information regarding use by subject area is considered in the formulation of the allocation of funds to academic departments.

Collection Weeding and Deselection. The head of acquisitions did not discard any items during the study period. Titles discarded by the head of reference were primarily superseded editions of reference works or materials no longer needed in the reference collection and were therefore transferred to the circulating collection. During the last week, some indexes and abstracting services were identified that would be discontinued because of spiraling costs and low use. Other candidates for discard were items that had been in the serials cataloging backlog for a long period of time and had never been added to the collections.

SUMMARY

Four academic libraries participated in the study. Two libraries were located in colleges and two were on university campuses. All were in close geographic proximity. There was a variety of organizational and budgetary structures. In all four libraries, all professional librarians could select materials for the collections, as well as any faculty member of the institution. Very different collection development programs ranged from informal to somewhat formal, with collection development policies that were, in three of the libraries, either in the process of being written or revised. The fourth library did not have a policy, simply a series of collection development statements.

7

Case Studies: Special Libraries

MEDICAL SCHOOL "A" LIBRARY

Organization

Location and Size. Medical School "A" Library is located on the grounds of a private medical college in a large metropolitan area. The collections are the result of a merger between the original college collection and the library of an unaffiliated Academy of Medicine to provide better service to patrons of both libraries.

The Medical School offers a degree of Doctor of Medicine and some post-graduate degrees in the basic sciences to a student body of over 700 individuals. There is a small hospital on the grounds of the Medical School for which the library provides services, and there are affiliate contracts with over 30 other hospitals in the immediate geographic area. The library must provide services to these hospitals, although most have libraries that serve the primary clinical needs of their own staff. In addition, health professionals not connected with the Medical School, the Academy of Medicine, or the hospitals may purchase an annual "membership" to the library, which affords them all the privileges of service and collections. Commercial firms and individuals who are not health professionals may also purchase memberships.

Organizational Structure. The director of the library reports to the dean of the medical school and is advised by the Library Board appointed by the president of the school (Figure 7.1). The director, as well as being the administrative head of the Medical School "A" Library, is also the primary selector for the collections. In addition, there is the assistant director and four professional librarians: head of reference services, head of technical services, head of interlibrary loan, and the regional medical library coordinator. There are eight staff members, totalling 14 employees of the library.

Physical Facility and Collection Size. The collections of approximately 121,000 items are housed in an 1,000 square foot facility with no room for expansion. There are, in addition to the monographs and serials, audio and visual media and some retrospective and special collections.

Budget

Of the $450,000 total budget received by the Medical School "A" Library during the year studied, $200,000 was budgeted for the purchase of materials for the collections. The money is received from a variety of sources, including state and local funds, gifts, user fees and memberships, and grants.

The library uses a line-item budget, with an amount allocated for collections according to the following plan: when the collection budget is given to the library at the start of the fiscal year, an amount is set aside for the invoice received from the subscription agent to cover the periodical subscription renewal costs for the following year, including a percentage additionally expected for price increases and foreign currency exchange rate increases. The remaining budget funds for collection development are then available for the purchase of monographs and requested audiovisual materials. At the time of this study, there were enough funds to purchase all requested material with the exception of titles in subject areas peripheral to the primary subject areas of the collections.

Collection Development Program

Medical School "A" Library has an informal collection development program. There is no collection development policy, although the director felt that one was necessary and would be developed in the near future.

Selection Responsibility. The director has primary responsibility for

Figure 7.1
Medical School "A" Library Organizational Chart

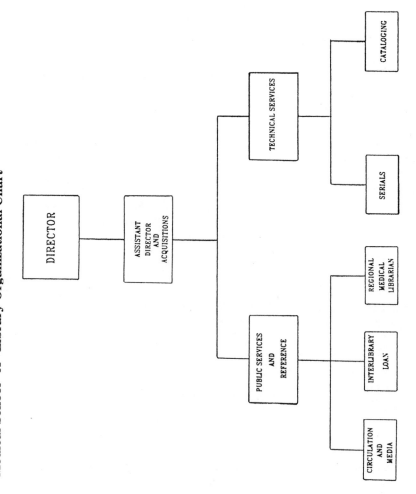

selection of materials at the Medical School "A" Library. He is aided by the assistant director and accepts requests of patrons for materials. Suggestions for purchases from the head of interlibrary loan and the regional medical library coordinator are bought whenever possible as well.

Selection Procedures. Requests from users and from staff are examined by the director and assistant director. The assistant director types order forms for the titles approved for purchase and sends the orders to appropriate vendors.

The head of technical services is, in fact, responsible only for serials including ordering, processing, check-in, and claiming. She does no cataloging and/or processing of other materials; these are handled by the assistant director.

Study Participants. Both the director and the assistant director agreed to participate in this research. The selectors stated that patron requests accounted for the majority of the titles they identified for purchase. Additional methods for identifying titles included:

1. listings of new books in publisher's advertisements
2. recommendations made by the Reference Department
3. vendor listings of new titles
4. new editions of the "Brandon list"[1]

Collection Evaluation. According to the director of the library, there have not been, nor are there planned, any evaluations of the collections. He said that the library does not buy enough materials for the collections each year to require such an evaluation. He also indicated that because of the shortage of personnel, there was no one who could be spared from other duties to conduct an evaluation. One use study had been conducted a few years prior to this study, however, it was a patron survey by the Interlibrary Loan Department and had no identifiable impact on the development of collections. No use studies are projected for the future.

Collection Weeding and Deselection. There is no weeding program, nor is there a policy on weeding for this library. During the study period, only one book was discarded—a biochemistry textbook that was in poor condition. A new copy of the same edition was ordered to replace the discarded title.

MEDICAL SCHOOL "B" LIBRARY

Organization

Location and Size. Medical School "B" is one campus of a multicampus private university, located in a major metropolitan area. The school's campus is surrounded by many health care facilities, some of which are affiliated with the university, and many Medical School "B" faculty hold joint appointments in the other health care facilities.

Medical School "B" campus includes schools of Medicine, Graduate Studies, Allied Health Sciences, and a Graduate School of Nursing with over 600 students. In another part of the city, there is a School of Dentistry campus of the university, and the small dental library is considered a branch of the Medical School "B" Library.

Organizational Structure. The director of the library is the administrator of the library's programs. The associate director is also designated as head of public services, with the reference librarian reporting to her. All other departments, including Circulation, Interlibrary Loan, Serials, Archives, Periodicals, and Technical Services, report directly to the director (Figure 7.2). Employees of the library include 8 professional librarians, 17 staff members, and 11 part-time student clerks and pages.

Physical Facility and Collection Size. Medical School "B" Library has 24,000 square feet in its main facility, with an additional 5,000 square feet of space available for expansion in other parts of the medical center. This space contains 137,000 volumes, with enough storage space for the next two to three years. The collections are comprised of print material only; there are no audio or visual media owned by the library.

Budget

The operational budget for the Medical School "B" Library during the study period was $850,000 of which $300,000 was designated to purchase materials for the collections. The majority of the funds is received from the parent university through Medical School "B," and it is unknown whether the funds are exclusively from tuition, or whether they include local, state, federal, grant, foundation, or fund-raising monies.

Collections funds are given to the library in a lump sum, without any breakdown for monographs or subscriptions. There is no procedure within the library for determining how much of the budget is spent proportionately for monographs or serials.

Additional collection funds are received from over 10 endowments that have been established to purchase materials in specified subject areas. The director has complete control of all endowment funds. All funds are spent for monographs, serials, and some retrospective materials.

Figure 7.2
Medical School "B" Library Organizational Chart

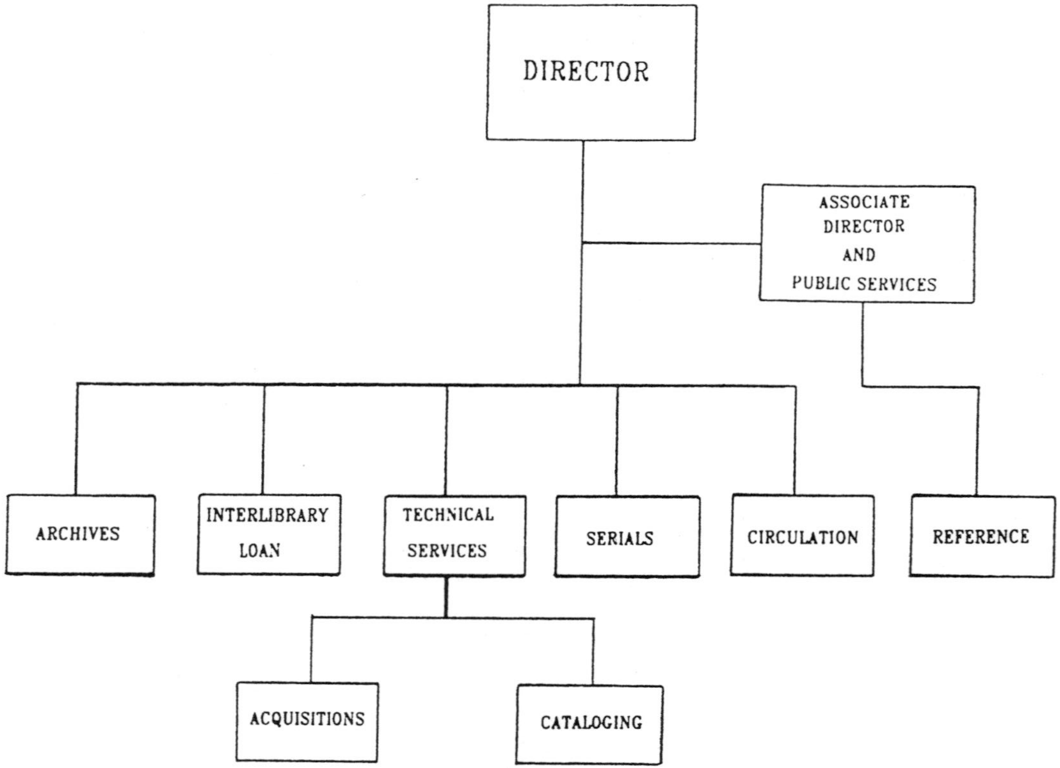

Collection Development Program

Although there is no collection development policy, the collection development program is structured and formal.

Selection Responsibility. The director is the selector for all the collections. He is aided in selecting materials by many of his library faculty. The associate director/head of public services and the reference librarian make many of the pre-selection decisions. They review the selection sources, interlibrary loan requests, and Library of Congress proofslips, and they mark any titles of potential interest, to bring them to the director's attention.

Selection Procedures. Any suggestions for purchase from these two faculty and from the public are sent to the director, who makes the final decisions regarding the purchase of titles. The director then forwards all approved titles to the order clerk for purchase. She types the order forms and sends them to various vendors or goes to the University Bookstore and purchases them for the library.

Study Participants. Three of the library faculty agreed to participate in this study: the director of the library, associate director/head of public services, and the reference librarian. The order clerk was interviewed on an irregular and occasional basis also.

Sources used to identify titles for purchase throughout the study period, in order of frequency, were:

1. patron requests for materials not already on order
2. Library of Congress proofslips
3. listings of new books in *Weekly Record*
4. publisher's advertisements

Collection Evaluation. There have been no evaluations of the collections and none are projected for the future. As the director said, "Who's going to do it?" He remarked that there is good feedback from the faculty of Medical School "B" about the usefulness of the collections, which he considers "encouraging" regarding the effectiveness of the collection development program. No use studies have been conducted either; statistics kept by the Circulation Department are not examined with the collections in mind.

Collection Weeding and Deselection. There is no active weeding or deselection program at the Medical School "B" Library. During the study period, the only titles discarded were previous editions of newly received titles. In addition, any titles reported lost were withdrawn from the collection's holdings, if they could not be replaced through vendors.

MEDICAL SCHOOL "C" LIBRARY

The state university system is composed of schools scattered throughout the state. Several of these schools specialize in medicine and allied health sciences.

Organization

Location and Size. Medical School "C" is part of a state university system. It is located in the southern part of the city and offers degree programs in medicine, nursing, allied health sciences, and graduate studies to almost 900 students. There is a hospital that is part of Medical School "C" and another hospital operated with public funds; the school's faculty members often have clinical appointments in both hospitals and students can gain clinical experience in the patient care settings of both hospitals.

The collections were created over a long period of time but increased dramatically with the merger of the original college and the local Academy of Medicine collections. Service is provided to the faculty, staff, and students of Medical School "C," and members of the local Medical Society and Dental Society.

Organizational Structure. The director of the library serves as the administrator of the library's programs. Reporting to him directly are the head of public services, who oversees the Reference, Circulation, and Interlibrary Loan Departments; the head of technical services, in charge of the Serials, Binding, and Cataloging Departments; and the head of media services (Figure 7.3). In total there are 14 professional employees and 21 staff or clerical workers.

Physical Facility and Collection Size. Located in the center of the medical campus, the library consists of 30,000 square feet, with approximately 10,000 square feet of storage space. There are 250,000 volumes in the collections and a steadily growing audio and visual media collection. The stacks were crowded and the storage space was almost full at the time of the study.

Budget

Medical School "C" Library received its $1 million budget from a variety of sources. The majority of the funds comes from the state university through the Office of Budget Control. Regional and county funds are given directly to the library, as well as any gift money the library might receive. There were some endowment funds available also. The collection budget is approximately 30 percent of the total budget, or $300,000.

Figure 7.3
Medical School "C" Library Organizational Chart

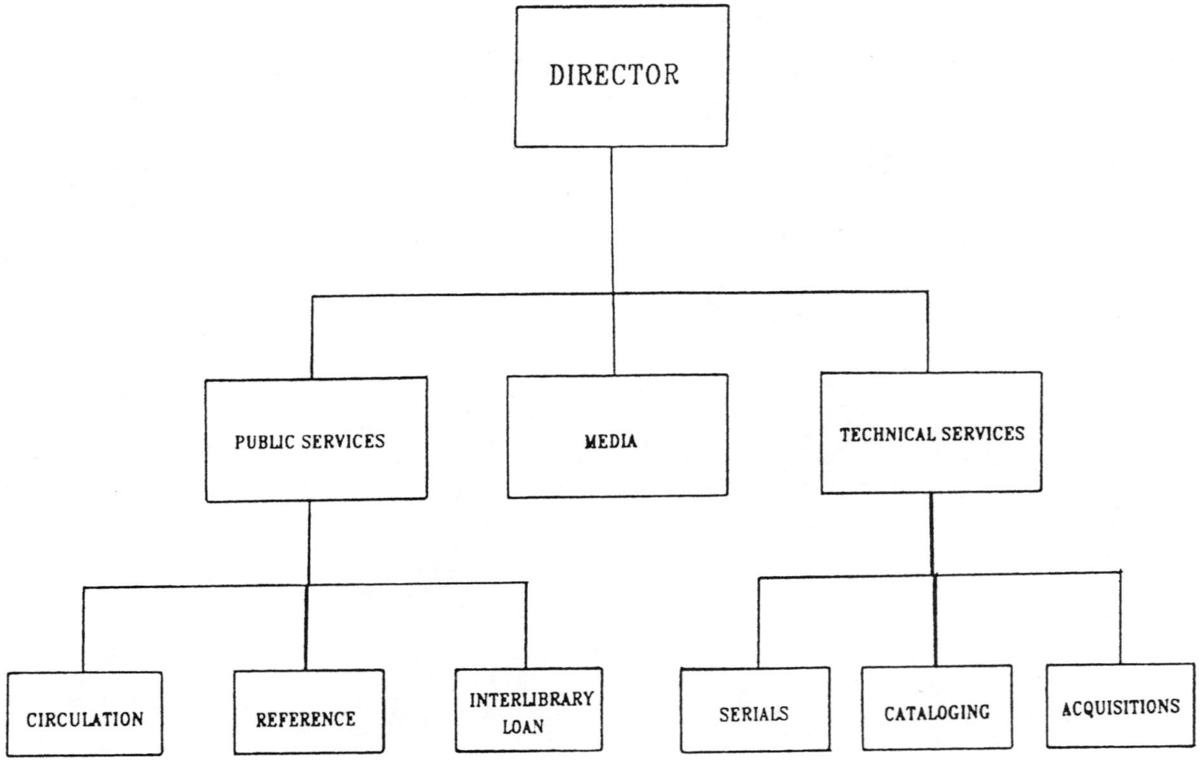

Collection funds are allocated for monographs, periodicals, serials, audio and visual media, and for the reference collection. Guidelines for amounts of expenditures are given to the selectors each fiscal year by the director of the library.

Collection Development Program

There is a loosely defined collection development program at the Medical School "C" Library. The knowledge of the selectors, combined with requests from patrons, are the bases for the program. There is no collection development policy, although a media selection policy, written by the head of media services, is under consideration.

Selection Responsibility. The head of public services has the responsibility to select all monographs, periodicals, and other printed material for the collections. Audio and visual material selection is the responsibility of the head of media services. Selection recommendations are made by the reference librarian and library patrons.

Selection Procedures. All requests for purchase from patrons, library staff, and others are reviewed by the head of public services. He forwards approved requests to the Technical Services Department, where orders are generated on the OCLC acquisitions subsystem or are typed by clerks and sent to publishers.

Study Participants. The head of public services and the head of media services participated in this study. The reference librarian, who has responsibility for selection of materials for the reference collection, was unavailable during the time of the study and could not be interviewed. There were occasional interviews with the director and the head of technical services.

Sources used to identify titles for purchase throughout the study period, in order of frequency, were:

1. patron requests for materials not already on order
2. publisher's advertisements
3. interlibrary loan requests

All recommended titles were purchased; no orders were rejected for purchase.

Collection Evaluation. No systematic evaluation of the monographic collection had been conducted in the past because there was no staff or time for such a project. However, the head of public services described his "nonsystematic" method of collection evaluation. He stated that "if the items on the shelves are in order, and in good shape, they haven't been read in a long time."

The Technical Services staff did conduct an evaluation of the periodicals subscriptions. The circulation records were examined for each title in the collection, and titles were identified that could be eliminated due to lack of usage.

Collection Weeding and Deselection. There is no written policy on weeding. As stated by the head of public services, "if there are tight spots in the shelving," then those areas are weeded for more room. He estimated that there is room for the current year for the storage of materials, but that without substantial weeding there would not be enough room for the next five years.

MEDICAL SCHOOL "D" LIBRARY

Organization

Location and Size. Medical School "D" is a component of a private university that has a limited number of campuses throughout the state. The main university campus is located in the northern part of the state, and houses the university's administrative offices. Medical School "D" is in the heart of the city, in close proximity to other affiliated health care facilities. It offers degree programs in medicine, nursing, and some allied health sciences. There is an affiliated hospital nearby. Service is provided to the faculty, staff, and approximately 400 students of Medical School "D," and to the research technicians and nurses who are affiliated with the medical school.

Organizational Structure. All departments of the library report to the director, the administrative head of the library, and who reports to the dean of the medical school. The director is advised in library policy matters by the Library Committee (Figure 7.4). There are 11 professional and 15 clerical employees.

Physical Facility and Collection Size. Medical Center "D" Library is located in the center of the medical school campus. It consists of approximately 17,000 square feet of space on four floors, housing almost 120,000 volumes. The collection consists of monographs, periodicals, serials, approval plan books, blanket orders, media, and special collections of historical material. There are some library personnel located in other parts of the campus, and there are no areas that have been identified as available for expansion of the collection or facility.

Budget

Funding for the library is received from a variety of sources. During the study period, the majority of the $800,000 annual budget came from the Medical School administration and from gifts and endow-

Figure 7.4
Medical School "D" Library Organizational Chart

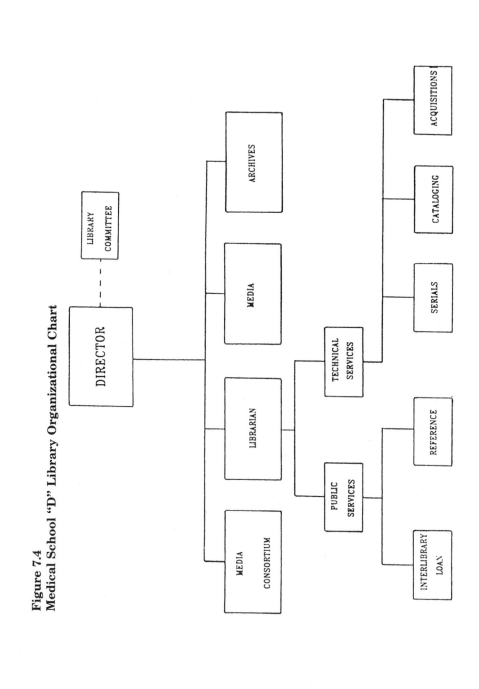

ments. Additional funding is provided through membership fees collected from affiliates. Subscribers pay at least $2,000 per year for the privilege of full use of the library's resources and services. It is unknown whether the funds given to the library by Medical School "D" are exclusively tuition, or include local, state, federal, grant, foundation, or fund-raising monies.

Over $250,000 of the budget is allocated for collections. Materials purchased include monographs, periodicals, serials, approval plan books, blanket orders, media, special collections, and reference materials. There is very little retrospective collecting, usually initiated and approved by the director. Allocations within these categories of materials are determined by the director in consultation with the respective selectors.

Collection Development Program

Medical School "D" Library has a structured and formal collection development program, with an extensive and detailed collection development policy (see Appendix J) and a well-defined acquisitions procedure manual. The policy was written within the previous five years by a consultant and select members of the staff.

Selection Responsibility. Generally, the primary responsibility for the collection development program rests with the head of technical services. However, at the time of this study, there was a major reorganization of the Technical Services Department and, due to problems in the Serials Section, the head of technical services could not devote time to selection. Therefore, the cataloger was assigned primary responsibility for monographic selection. The cataloger, who did not have any experience in collection development, was in the process of learning the needs and procedures of the collection development program.

Assisting the selectors was the acquisitions assistant, whose duties involved the maintenance of order records, and the acceptance or rejection of books received on the approval plan from a local book vendor. Several reference librarians and the document delivery librarian also assisted the selectors by recommending titles for purchase.

Selection Procedures. There are several methods by which monographic materials are selected for the collections. One method in use is an approval plan by which the library received all newly published monographs that qualify for shipment according to the vendor's profile. These shipments are examined by the acquisitions assistant according to the specifications of the collection development policy, and all monographs that do not meet the criteria in the policy are returned to the vendor. Materials that do meet the criteria are then divided into two categories: monographs that the library will buy and monographs that need expert evaluation. The library has a number of consultants on the faculty of Medical School "D" who are willing to examine approval books within their areas of subject specialty and make recommendations regarding the purchase status of such monographs. The monographs are forwarded to the experts and are then returned with recommendations. Those books suggested for purchase are kept; the others are returned.

Requests from library faculty, staff, and users are accepted by the Technical Services Department. All requests are examined by either the head of technical services or the cataloger, and those approved for purchase are forwarded to the acquisitions assistant. She types the orders and sends them to the appropriate vendor or publisher, or tries to identify local bookstores that stock the title if it is a rush order.

Study Participants. The head of technical services, the cataloger, and the acquisitions assistant all participated in this study. The most frequent methods for identifying titles for purchase were:

1. patron requests for materials not already on order
2. approval plan books
3. recommendations from librarians
4. interlibrary loan requests
5. listings of new books in publisher's advertisements
6. bibliographies and reviewing sources

Collection Evaluation. The collections are regularly evaluated by the Reference Department, and recommendations for weeding and for purchases are forwarded to the head of technical services or the cataloger. These evaluations are expected to continue on a regular basis.

About five years prior to this research, a study of the use of the periodicals collection was conducted. As a result of this use study, many periodical titles that had not been circulated for a number of years were discontinued. There were no use studies projected for the future.

Collection Weeding and Deselection. There is a written policy on weeding, but it does not appear in the collection development policy. It is, rather, in the "Cataloger's Manual." Its provisions are that duplicates of monographs are weeded, and all earlier editions of a text with the exception of two previous editions held by the library, plus the first edition. This weeding is done automatically by the catalogers when a new edition of a text is received. Two years prior to this research, an inventory of the collections was taken, and all second copies of currently held texts were discarded. The library no longer purchases multiple copies of monographs and subscribes to very few duplicate copies of periodicals. During the study period, outdated reference titles and two "ruined" books were discarded.

SUMMARY

The special libraries chosen for this research were medical school libraries. The only common factors among the four libraries were their subject matter, the geographic location, and the fact that they were connected with educational institutions. Otherwise, the libraries were very different in organizational structure, budget, and collection development programs. Three did not have collection development policies, and one did. Two directors, one head of public services, and one head of technical services were assigned primary responsibility for the development of the collections.

NOTE

1. "Brandon list" or "Brandon-Hill list" refer to a biennial listing of books considered essential to small medical libraries. This listing is commonly published in an April issue of the *Bulletin of the Medical Library Association.*

8

Areas of Concern to Libraries

Throughout the investigations of selectors' decision making in various types of libraries, certain concerns were apparent. These concerns are universal in impact and affect the decisions of most of the selectors. Therefore, it is important to identify and examine the potential effect these concerns may have on any library situation.

BUDGET ALLOCATION

The manner in which the budget was allocated for the library had a major impact on the development of the collections in all the libraries studied. Of primary importance to all selectors was the amount of monies allotted for collection development. In many cases, a surplus of funds allocated for other areas of library operation, such as personnel or supplies, could not be transferred to collection development.

In three of the public libraries, budgets were encumbered or expended during the study period and selectors slowed or ceased their selection decision making until the new fiscal year. This meant that at least two to three months of information on new materials available for collections would, at best, be briefly scanned and items for purchase added to a desiderative file for future purchase. The selectors in the fourth public library were encouraged to spend the remaining budgeted funds immediately. This required quick identification of materials that might be appropriate for the collections and, in some cases, the selectors did not have time to consider their selections carefully because of other job duties and pressures.

Budgets were the main motivating factor in collection development for all four school libraries. Due to inadequate funds, increasing book costs, and expensive computer software, the librarians carefully spent their funds. Since each librarian had stated her desire for quality, she weighed each decision of need against cost while trying to maintain organizational and accreditation standards for the number of books per child without forsaking quality. The budget program in each school played a direct role in the collection development program, especially in requiring percentages of funds to be spent on books and audiovisual materials. Some flexibility was permitted in the three schools at which funds could be transferred to a needed area of the budget, and collection money could be augmented with gifts and fund raising.

In academic libraries, of primary importance to all selectors was the amount of monies allotted for collection development. In all four academic libraries, budgets were encumbered or expended during the study period and selectors slowed or ceased their selection decision making until the new fiscal year. This meant that at least two to five months of information on new materials available for collections would, at best, be briefly scanned and items for purchase added to a desiderative file for future purchase, as in the public libraries.

In all four medical school libraries, the budget was also of primary importance to the selectors. The problems caused by inflation, combined with decreasing increments in the library budget, forced the seletors to be much more selective in their purchases for the collections than they had been previously. In the past, selectors could purchase materials that filled an obvious need, although the item might not have been of the highest quality. However, with the decrease in spending power, selectors felt that they must be more concerned with the quality of the material. In addition, materials that presented information of wide appeal to the patrons of the institution were purchased in preference to high quality but narrow scope materials when funds were limited. Surplus funds allocated for other areas of library operations by the institution could not be used for collection development. Extra funds were available to all libraries through gifts, endowments, or fund-raising programs, but the amount of money fluctuated. Two libraries had programs in which unaffiliated individuals or institutions could purchase "memberships" in the library that permitted them to have full use of collections and services. The "membership" monies could be used to augment collection budgets.

SUPPORT OF THE MISSION AND GOALS OF THE INSTITUTION

In all of the libraries, the written or unwritten goals of the collection development programs are to provide as much material as possible within the limits of the budget and to meet the needs of the patrons. These goals are generally stated in terms of the extent to which the library will support the education, research, recreational, or other needs of the patrons or the institution.

In the public libraries, each of the selectors stated an awareness and familiarity with the goals, mission, and objectives of their libraries. They indicated that the materials selected for purchase for the collections were compatible with those goals, missions, and objectives.

In each school, the librarian stated that all materials purchased were essential to the curriculum and complemented the mission, goals, and objectives of the educational programs. Providing quality educational/instructional materials was a high priority in each librarian's mind. Statements of the goals, mission, and objectives of the schools were available in the written collection development policies for each school (see Appendices E, F, and H) and formed a framework that was accepted by the four librarians. They each tried to meet those goals and objectives in a timely fashion, although sometimes daily job requirements prohibited them from doing so.

Support of the mission and goals of the academic institutions was the second most important area of concern identified by the selectors in all four academic libraries. All selectors demonstrated an awareness of the new issues and concerns of their patrons and shared a desire to purchase library materials that would appropriately meet those needs. Each of the selectors stated an awareness and familiarity with the goals, mission, and objectives of their libraries and indicated that the materials selected for purchase for the collections were compatible with those goals, missions, and objectives.

In all four medical school libraries, the goals of the collection development programs, although not expressed in written terms, were to provide as much material as possible within the limits of each institution's budget to meet the needs of the students, researchers, and staff members of the medical schools or affiliated health science institutions. These needs included education, research, and patient care. All selectors were acutely aware of changes in the curricula of their educational institutions. They were also familiar with the research needs in the institution and attempted to purchase materials to support the on-going research of the faculty and staff. Patient care was supported through the acquisition of clinical materials, although purchase of clinical materials was de-emphasized because of budgetary constraints.

STANDARDS AND GUIDELINES

Standards and guidelines are hailed in the literature as essential yardsticks by which library collections can be measured and evaluated. Few authors have offered methodologies by which standards can be applied to "typical" library collections, perhaps because no one has been able to develop a definition of a "typical library." Since the primary purpose of a library, or information center, is to provide the materials and services needed by a particular clientele and since any given group of individuals that may constitute a clientele differ from any other group, it seems obvious that the materials and services will have to differ too. If, then, the materials and services differ, so too will the collections. It also seems obvious that there cannot be a definition of a "typical library." Even within similar types of libraries (i.e., public, school, and academic), the mission, institution, and clientele combine to create unique information needs that require different collections to meet them.

Attempts have been made by various organizations to develop standards for certain types of libraries. In most cases, these standards are to be applied to libraries supporting educational programs and are designed to identify minimal levels of quantity of materials expected to adequately serve curricular and research needs. For public libraries, and for some types of special libraries not serving educational programs, guidelines have been developed to provide a foundation for collection development programs; standards are not possible because of the variations in the libraries, clienteles, and collections.

The guidelines for collections in public libraries are very general. None of the selectors expressed a concern with any guidelines, such as those developed by the American Library Association.[1] Several selectors mentioned an awareness of bibliographies and lists that contained recommended materials for public library collections, and they attempted to purchase appropriate materials from those lists.

There were guidelines and standards applicable to each school. Each librarian stated that she followed guidelines and standards handed down by the school system. Other guidelines and standards were created by local, state, federal, and national agencies for school libraries. Some standards had to be met in order to maintain accreditation or to receive federal funding. Some guidelines were created by principals and teachers, with input from the media specialist or librarian.

There are a number of standards and/or guidelines for collections in academic libraries, developed by the Association of College and

Research Libraries.[2] None of the selectors expressed a concern with meeting any of the existing standards except in relation to accreditation visits. Several selectors reviewed bibliographies and lists that contain recommended materials for academic library collections and purchased titles from those lists.

The standards established by the Joint Commission on the Accreditation of Hospitals (now known as the Joint Commission on Accreditation of Healthcare Organizations) were of importance to the medical school librarians.[3] All four libraries attempted to conform to the standards for library service required by the accrediting teams of the Liaison Committee on Medical Education.[4] These standards vary according to the educational programs under review for re-accreditation. In addition, the libraries attempted to meet the standards for library service in the accreditation processes of the Council on Dental Accreditation of the American Dental Association, the National League for Nursing, the Council on Education for the American Occupational Therapy Association, the National Association of Physical Therapists, and the American Council on Pharmaceutical Education, wherever applicable. There are no collection development guidelines followed by any of the selectors, although one selector said that he attempts to have copies of all titles that appear on the "Brandon list"[5] in the library.

NETWORKING AND RESOURCE SHARING

The evolution of technologically sophisticated communications systems has dramatically altered the nature of networking and resource sharing since the early 1960s. Bulky packages sent through the postal service, and perhaps damaged or lost, were unsatisfactory. Besides, the lending library had to do without the book or journal until it could be returned, and patrons would complain. The photocopier provided a simple means to share printed works with libraries that did not have copies of the original and could not afford them, while still satisfying patron needs. Telefacsimile equipment provides an even faster method of sharing information and materials by enabling a lending library to instantaneously provide needed items to a requesting library, anywhere in the world.

The computerized communications networks, as availability and use increased and prices decreased, provided quick, easy, interactive, and accurate information exchange mechanisms. These networks are seen, by the library profession, as attractive alternatives to the traditional process of attempting to purchase all materials that might be needed by their patrons. Unfortunately, most of the libraries surveyed for this research did not have the funds, equipment, or personnel with expertise, to take advantage of the new technology. Many of the libraries were still using traditional methods of resource sharing.

While all four public libraries belonged to interlibrary loan networks, only one of the selectors mentioned that selection decisions were affected by the fact that materials could be borrowed elsewhere. Some of the selectors did not know what was in the collections of other departments or branches within their own library systems.

The use of available alternate resources was not extensive in the four school libraries studied. The county school used interlibrary loan. The Central Processing Center of the city school system used resource-sharing networks such as OCLC,[6] but the two city school libraries had no direct contact with the networks. The two city schools and the county school participated in informal cooperative programs with a neighboring city public library.

Selectors in three of the academic libraries mentioned that their selection decisions were influenced by the fact that materials could be borrowed elsewhere. The three libraries are members of a local consortium, developed in order for member libraries to share resources, including collections and services. Participation in this consortium enabled the selectors to avoid purchasing expensive titles that had the potential of only occasional use in their own libraries, and also to avoid duplication of such titles in the region.

The selectors in all four medical school libraries expressed a great awareness of the positive effect of network membership. All four libraries were part of the Regional Medical Library Program (RMLP) of the National Library of Medicine.[7] Two of the libraries were designated as resource libraries for the RMLP. The third had a role as a collector of some endangered titles (titles that were expensive, specialized, and likely to be eliminated from the collections of other libraries in the area). The fourth, as well as being a member of the RMLP, was an affiliate member of a media consortium that was active for a period of time in the region. Unfortunately, the media consortium dissolved and the library found that some of the monograph collection funds were required to develop an audiovisual collection. This same library was a member of an interinstitutional library consortium that had developed a cooperative collection development plan, in which designated institutions collected titles in specific subject areas and made them available to other members of the consortium and to their patrons. In this way, the library could be more selective about the titles it purchased for its collections.

COLLECTION DEVELOPMENT POLICIES

An accepted theory of librarianship is that libraries cannot have adequate and appropriate collections to meet patron needs without having collection development policies. Since such a policy should have a definition and assessment of the collections, the community and its needs, and any resource-sharing associations available to the library, it can be used to provide continuity in developing the needed materials and services to meet the mission, goals, and objectives of the library program. Without such a policy, the selectors have the responsibility to develop collections without the background information available to do the job effectively. Those selectors who have experience in developing collections are aware of the types of information they need and develop a knowledge base over a period of time that allows them to be effective in selection decisions. Selectors without such experience, or who are new to a library, do not have that background and must spend a good deal of their time learning their library's philosophies, collections, and clientele. Good collection development policies not only provide a picture of the collections and a plan for their continued development, but they can be used as training tools for future collection development personnel.

Many librarians have not had, or taken, the time to create such policies. Often, selectors cannot cite the collection development policy of their library, if there is one, although they may be able to identify written or unwritten selection or acquisitions policies. Such policies will often indicate approved information sources from which to select material or acceptable supply sources from which to buy selected items, but these are only parts of the whole. Collection development is more than identifying a title to purchase or choosing a publisher or wholesaler from whom to acquire the title. For libraries that do not invest the time and effort to create a collection development policy, expensive and time-consuming training periods will be needed to develop knowledgeable personnel.

Two of the public libraries had written collection development policies, partially reproduced in Appendices C and D. One library had a written selection policy only (Appendix A) and a committee was writing a policy for the fourth. Only one selector, working in the library without a policy, stated that a set of written standards created for selection of a particular type of material (see Appendix B) was continually in mind when making selection decisions. None of the other selectors mentioned the collection development or selection policy when identifying their thought processes in selecting or not selecting materials for purchase. Nevertheless, the selectors all seemed to use the same criteria with regard to the purchase of material for the collections.

In the schools, there were written policies for developing the collections, as required by the accrediting agencies, including policies for weeding and gifts (see Appendices E through I). Each school librarian followed unwritten policies concerning duplicates and replacements;

these unwritten policies were created by the librarian through her expertise and her own discretion.

One of the academic libraries had a written collection development policy (see Appendix I). One college and one university library had collection development or selection policies that were so outdated, inadequate, or irrelevant to the current program of the libraries that the policies were no longer followed. The fourth academic library, in a university, did not have a collection development policy or a librarywide selection policy. Instead, selection policy statements for some disciplines were developed by departments and schools on the campus. None of the selectors in academic libraries mentioned collection development or selection policies, current or outdated, influencing their thought processes while making selection decisions.

Of the four medical school libraries, three did not have collection development or selection policies, although such policies were planned for the near future. The fourth library had both collection development (see Appendix J) and acquisitions policies.

Interestingly, only one of the selectors mentioned the selection policy when identifying his thought processes in selecting or not selecting materials for purchase. None of the others mentioned any of the written policies, although they did describe some unwritten policies. They all seemed to use the same criteria with regard to the purchase of material for the collections, including format of the materials, subject matter, level of presentation, copyright date, price, and availability of the same information in other materials already in the collections.

SELECTION METHODS

Selectors in all the libraries studied had favorite selection sources that they regularly consulted for information about new materials to add to their collections. In the public, school, and academic libraries these sources were consulted because they had consistently provided reviews that coincided with the opinions of either the selector or the patrons of the library. In the special libraries, currency of information was paramount, and the selectors were concerned with the speed with which the source listed newly published items, rather than with reviews of the items.

All selectors in the public libraries stated that requests for purchase of materials were accepted and welcome from library patrons and members of their staffs. Formal and informal user studies played an important role in the decision making of the selectors in public libraries.

Each school librarian accepted requests from all patrons, including anyone connected with students or the institution. Satisfying student needs and providing quality educational/instructional materials was a high priority in each librarian's mind. Each librarian also realized the importance of maintaining good relations with all patrons and trying to satisfy as many of the needs presented to her as possible. Each exhibited a good working relationship with students, faculty, staff, and parents when observed during the study.

All selectors in the academic libraries stated that requests for the purchase of materials were accepted and welcomed from library patrons and members of their staffs. Continual formal and informal user studies were as important in the academic libraries as in the public libraries.

Common to all four medical school libraries was the acceptance of requests from faculty, staff, and students of the institutions which they served. Aside from those requests, recommendations were also accepted from library faculty and staff and were sought from the members of the reference departments in the libraries.

Selectors in all libraries described personal subject prejudices that influenced their decision making during the study period. These were subject prejudices that the selectors felt were justifiable in the decision not to purchase an item for the collections because of their experience and their contact with the patrons, as well as personal dislike or distaste for certain subjects.

SUMMARY

It is evident that for the libraries studied the most important issue affecting selectors' decision making in any of the types of libraries was the amount of money available for purchasing material. On occasion, there could have been enough money in the library's budget to meet collection purchasing needs, but that money was assigned to a dedicated budget line that could not be used for collection materials. Related to the amount of funds was the problem of ensuring that all budget funds were encumbered before purchasing employees closed the books for the fiscal year.

Second in importance, according to the selectors, was support of the mission, goals, and objectives of the institution and/or library. Selectors stated an awareness of the mission and goals of the libraries, and they believed that their selections for the collections supported those missions and goals.

Standards were of importance to libraries that were part of institutions required to undergo accreditation by some educational or professional organization. However, the standards were of concern primarily during the accreditation process. They were generally not considered during the selection of materials unless the accreditating agency identified specific areas needing attention before re-accreditation could be achieved. Guidelines were generally not considered during the selection process.

Three academic and all medical school libraries that participated in this research were aware of, and users of, networking and resource-sharing consortia. The small college library and the school libraries were occasional users of interlibrary loan networks; the public libraries were moderate users. It appears that at present research-oriented institutions benefit the most from resource sharing and networking.

All selectors expressed the need for collection development policies and understood their worth. However, few had policies available in their libraries. Those that did have such policies available, regardless of library type, did not discern any impact of the policies on their decision making.

Finally, with regard to methods by which selectors identified materials for purchase, all selectors stated that they received requests for materials from patrons of the library. Also, all selectors had favorite sources they used to identify new titles for purchase.

NOTES

1. American Library Association, *Guidelines for Collection Development*, (Chicago: ALA, 1979).

2. The Association of College & Research Libraries has developed a number of standards for college and university libraries, including standards for the size of collections. These standards can be found in issues of *College & Research Libraries News*.

3. "Professional library service," *Accreditation Manual for Hospitals* (Chicago: Joint Commission on Accreditation of Hospitals, 1986), p. 211–214. The Joint Commission on Accreditation of Hospitals is now known as the Joint Commission on Accreditation of Healthcare Organizations (JCAHO) and published the latest edition of the manual in 1988.

4. The Liaison Committee on Medical Education is sponsored by the Association of American Medical Colleges and the Council on Medical Education of the American Medical Association.

5. A biennial listing of books considered essential to small medical libraries. This listing is commonly published in an April issue of the *Bulletin of the Medical Library Association*.

6. Online Computer Library Center, Incorporated produces one of the largest online bibliographic databases of materials available in library collections. It is commonly used to provide cataloging records

and for interlibrary loan information. Because of the size of the da-
tabase and the number and variety of contributing libraries, a national catalog has been developed that can be used for myriad purposes.

7. The Regional Medical Library Program, created by the Medical
Library Assistance Act (PL89-291) in 1965, provides a structure within
which health science libraries operate.

PART III
CONCLUSION

9

Dynamic Factors Affecting the Decision-Making Process

The decision-making process involves more than just consciously or unconsciously synthesizing all the information, experiences, and situations that an individual encounters throughout life. It is apparent that any decision making is influenced by both internal and external forces.

Internal forces include experience, expertise, training, and common sense—all attributes that an individual develops over a period of time and many of which cannot be taught. Some of these attributes can be learned by selectors through the use of well-designed policy statements and substantial training programs. The libraries studied, however, did not have training programs for selectors. Rather, the selectors were expected to use their knowledge and experience to develop the necessary background for selection decisions for the collections.

External forces that impact any decision process include the environment in which the decision maker is located and the circumstances prevalent during the time the decision is made. It is apparent that selectors made decisions because of, not in spite of, current financial and other situations in their libraries. For example, as the budgets were depleted, many selectors ceased examining the sources used to identify new titles because they could not have purchased any items they wanted. There was the expectation that, by the time funds were again released, the material would be outdated or no longer available commercially. Once the new fiscal year began, those selectors would review the sources they had ignored and make some selections. Other selectors continued to examine selectioᴜ sources and build a file of desired titles for order when new funds were released. As soon as funds were available, the selectors sent large orders that included the titles identified during the end of the previous fiscal year. Some selectors reviewed the file of titles prior to actually ordering, and found that sometimes they changed their minds and did not order items originally targeted for acquisition.

It would be interesting to know whether those titles originally selected and then rejected for purchase would have been used by the patrons of the library. This research did not deal with that issue. It would also be interesting to know whether those items wanted for the collections, but not available by the time the orders were sent, would have been needed by the patrons. Such a research project would be difficult to design and would take a long period of time to complete, but it would be possible.

Additional factors affected selectors' decision making. The factors identified in these studies can be categorized according to the framework developed by Mintzberg, Raisinghani, and Théorêt,[1] and described in Chapter 3.

INTERRUPTS

Interrupts are defined by Mintzberg, Raisinghani, and Théorêt as factors that are "caused by environmental forces."[2] These environmental forces may include job-related occurrences, personal needs, or other situations that may interrupt the planned work-flow for the selector.

Each selector was asked to identify what interruptions affected his/her decision making for collection development each week during the study period. Responses by the selectors can be categorized as follows.

Capital Constraints. Essential to the building of library collections is the amount of money available to purchase materials. Selectors should be able to depend on, and account for, funds budgeted for their areas of responsibility. Many of the selectors interviewed, however, could not state how much money remained in the accounts identified for their use, nor did they know how much they had spent during the fiscal year. Therefore, they were discomfited to learn there were no funds left in their budgets. Additionally, at times selectors were told by their administrators that budgeted funds were to be diverted from collections to be used in areas of "greater need" for the library.

In the public libraries, selectors in three of the institutions were notified that funds were expended and orders would be held until the next fiscal year unless there was an emergency purchase needed. The school media specialists in the four schools had limited funds and were required to meet an ordering deadline three months into the school year.

For all the academic libraries, the fiscal year was drawing to a close and the selectors were faced with identifying only essential materials for purchase. Disagreement with the records of the Purchasing Department caused some delay in the ability to purchase materials in one library, and most of the selectors found that they had to re-evaluate a number of items they wanted and forward only those they deemed of immediate need. The rest were to be held until the new budget was approved.

Several of the selectors in the special libraries identified capital constraints. One institution, for example, experienced a major problem in purchasing materials for the collections because the state legislature had not approved the state budget and, as a state institution, the library had no funds. Another special library had neared the limit for purchases and had a number of requests for materials that would have to be held until the next fiscal year.

These capital constraints obviously had an impact on the collection development decision making of these selectors. Ideally, selectors should have unlimited funding, so they may purchase all materials that would be useful for all patrons of the library. Since unlimited funding is an unrealistic dream, selectors must temper their best judgment with the realization that their funds are limited. While much can be purchased for the collections if published in the early months of a fiscal year, many important items may be missed if publishers release them later. Therefore, awareness of the publishing cycles is important if selectors want to take best advantage of their funding, and if they want to avoid capital constraints.

Unexpected Constraints. Occasionally, situations occur that are totally unexpected and that may affect the decision process. Generally these unexpected situations cannot be avoided through planning. In some cases, however, proper planning and/or training of personnel can aid the selectors in avoiding such unexpected constraints.

Two selectors in public libraries identified unexpected constraints in the creation of purchase orders for materials because typists were unavailable or did not pick up the material for typing. A third selector mentioned that the computer printer used for the creation of orders was needed for a special project and was unavailable for printing orders.

No unexpected constraints were observed in the school libraries.

Selectors in three of the academic libraries, however, encountered problems with lost orders, assumed to have been sent and later found misplaced. The material represented by these orders had to be re-evaluated in terms of whether the items were still desired for the library.

The special libraries' selectors often encountered unexpected constraints. For example, the primary book vendor for one library de-clared bankruptcy, resulting in problems with maintaining the stand-ing orders and with outstanding orders for which there were no status reports. In another library, the selector encountered problems with returning unwanted approval books because specialists examining those books did not honor the deadline for return of the materials. A selec-tor reported an unexpected constraint in the receipt of materials be-cause an order to a vendor was lost in transit, and extensive tele-phoning and a trace at the post office were required. Another unexpected constraint, identified by a selector, occured when a pub-lisher would not honor an order because of an outstanding bill not paid by the Purchasing Department.

Political Impasse. When the decision process is blocked by inside or outside groups, a political impasse might occur. Such an impasse oc-curred in one public library when a member of the library's board campaigned to have the library purchase fewer audiovisual and pa-perback books and more best sellers. No political impasses were ob-served in the school or academic libraries.

Only one special library selector identified a political impasse in the selection and acquisition of materials. The problem occurred when attempting to purchase audiovisual materials within the budgetary policies of a state-supported institution. The "overabundance of pa-perwork" required by the Purchasing Department was cited as a cause for the problems encountered by the selector.

TIMING DELAYS AND SPEEDUPS

As stated by Mintzberg, Raisinghani, and Théorêt, "Timing is ap-parently a major factor in strategic decision making, yet it has hardly been studied. . . . "[3] Delaying a selection decision may be of help while waiting for additional time, funds, or information, while speed-ing up the process may enable selectors to take advantage of special discounts or provide materials in emergency situations. However, it seems that most timing delays or speedups identified by these selec-tors were caused by outside factors such as patron needs, job duties, or decisions made by the administration of the institution.

Timing Delays. Significant timing delays during the decision-mak-ing process were identified by most of the selectors participating in these studies. For example, in the public libraries the selectors were interrupted by a number of scheduling delays. All selectors identified telephone calls, reference desk or other job duties, and patron queries or problems as causing time delays. Most selectors also cited delays in selection of materials caused by administrative duties, program planning, committee work or professional meetings, staff training or shortages, and visitors to the library.

Selectors in the school libraries identified a number of timing delays, some of which may be unique to this type of library. For example, selectors cited fire drills and unscheduled classes as delaying the decision-making process, interrupting their planned time for selection of materials. Additionally, built-in timing delays were needed for other job duties, such as bus and cafeteria monitoring; equipment setup, training, and use; telephone calls; professional meetings; and visitors to the library.

In the academic libraries, timing delays were caused by a number of situations: telephone calls, administrative duties, committee work, and personnel problems. Several also mentioned staff shortages and training, other job duties, and visitors to the library.

The selectors in special libraries identified the following timing delays (in order of frequency): telephone calls, reference desk or public service duties, professional meetings, personnel problems, correspondence needing immediate attention, administrative or other job duties, staff shortages or training, visitors to the library, and assorted other problems.

Speedups. A few situations occurred in three of the public libraries that required a speedup of the decision process, and those were primarily instances when material was needed immediately. Telephone orders or visits to bookstores resolved the problems. One public library was faced with the perplexing problem that the fiscal year was drawing to a close and there was still too much money in the budget, so orders had to be developed and sent before the bookkeeping process came to an end for the year. Other than rush requests for needed materials, there were no identifiable situations in the school or academic libraries that caused a speedup of the decision process.

Rush requests for materials occurred in several of the special libraries. The decision-making process was speeded up by the requestor's immediate need for material and special arrangements had to be made. Four selectors had to purchase the items at local bookstores and have them processed immediately. Prepublication options were also a factor in the acquisition of materials in two special libraries.

FEEDBACK DELAYS

While awaiting the results of a previous action, the decision maker may experience feedback delays. Feedback delays in two public libraries occurred primarily because selection tools that were circulated throughout the system did not reach the selector in a timely fashion. Therefore, in at least one case, several books ordered from one of the delayed selection tools were out-of-print. One other feedback delay identified during the study was the notification to a selector that a book ordered over six months earlier had not been received; a decision to reorder needed to be made.

No feedback delays were noted in school or academic libraries. The only occurrences of feedback delays in special libraries were in the library that had an approval plan. Books were examined by consultants to the library who sometimes failed to return the books by the designated time. This examination process delayed the clearance of invoices or return of unwanted materials until the recommendations were received.

SUMMARY

Within the framework of dynamic factors affecting decision making developed by Mintzberg, Raisinghani, and Théorêt, six factors were identified: interrupts, scheduling delays, feedback delays, timing delays and speedups, comprehension cycles, and failure recycles. Three of these dynamic factors seem to have little relevance to collection development decision making, since they are primarily appropriate to corporate and management decision making, as defined by these authors: scheduling delays (to allow complex decisions to be handled in manageable steps); comprehension cycles (which cause the decision process to cycle back to an earlier phase); and failure recycles (when there are no acceptable solutions and decisions are delayed until acceptable solutions can be found or criteria can be changed).[4]

Three dynamic factors can be identified in the decision process for selecting materials for library collections: interrupts (in the decision process); timing delays and speedups (to take advantage of special circumstances or await support or better conditions); and feedback delays (while the decision maker awaits the results of a previous action). One or more of these factors were cited by each of the selectors as having an impact on their decision making.

While many examples of these factors mentioned by the selectors were caused by external forces and could not be controlled, there were some examples that *could* be controlled with planning. For example, if selectors were given the opportunity to schedule their time for selection without being interrupted by the telephone or by patron problems or requests, they could take less time to make decisions. Then selected titles could be ordered and added to the collections with speed. Also, interrupts caused by capital constraints could be avoided if selectors were given, and accepted, responsibility for control over the money in the budget designated for their areas of the collections. They could then take advantage of the special situations or avoid some timing delays.

In summary, dynamic factors that influence the decision-making process of every selector in every library should be identified. Once identified, the factors should be examined to see what occurrences could be controlled and what situations could be enhanced or eliminated to make the job of the selector more efficient or effective.

NOTES

1. Henry Mintzberg, Duru Raisinghani, and André Théorêt, "The Structure of 'Unstructured' Decision Processes," *Administrative Science Quarterly* 21 (June 1976): 246–275.

2. Ibid., p. 263.

3. Ibid., p. 265.

4. Ibid., p. 264–266.

10

The Decision-Making Process

What does all this mean to the selector for a library collection? Does it have any effect on the daily work of collection developers? If most selectors are like those who were interviewed during the studies in the various types of libraries, there are several lessons to be learned about how they make decisions and what affects those decisions.

First, it seems that selectors are unsure about what they do when they select materials for libraries. Once their training period is over, and selectors become familiar with their libraries and the collections over which they have responsibility, selection of materials becomes routine. Remember Simon, who writes about conscious and unconscious decisions?[1] For the selectors, selection becomes an unconscious decision-making habit of which they are no longer aware. It resembles the trained habits that most people develop, like touch typing or opening a door. When asked how they reach selection decisions, selectors will often say that years of experience have provided them with the background and they "can just tell when something will fit the collection and the interests" of their patrons. Yet, when asked in a structured and repetitive manner, selectors became aware of all the thought processes at work during their selection decision making. In many cases, selectors participating in these studies not only became aware of what they thought and why they thought it, but also gained confidence that their selection decisions were valid and based upon relevant information.

Second, habits can sometimes become ingrained and continue when the need for them ceases. Unless one is aware of the habit, one cannot evaluate its usefulness. Occasionally habits need to be re-evaluated and changed. Reasons for selecting types of materials for a library's collection might not be the same during every decade, or even during each year. Library clientele changes; communities change; curricula change; and services offered by the library change. Selectors must be aware of any current or potential changes that may affect the information needs of patrons. Such changes can be identified through formal means, such as community analyses, or through informal means, such as selector awareness of the information mentally processed in recommending materials for purchase.

Third, many people are unaware of the process of decision making. This process has been studied for many years by individuals involved in research to develop more efficient or effective administrative and behavioral development. Much of what has been discovered by these researchers has had a positive impact on behavior and has also aided in the more effective deployment of individuals in corporate settings. The decision process and the factors that affect that process have provided administrators with the information necessary to operate effectively.

The library, too, can benefit from the lessons learned by these researchers. Many library administrators who are part of the corporate setting have learned this, perhaps painfully, in their attempts to maintain the corporate library as a viable and integral part of the company, well funded and secure. In corporations, most departments that do not seem to return value for money spent are quickly dissolved. Some special libraries have succumbed to such corporate decision making, while others thrive and grow. Administrators of successful corporate libraries seem to understand the decision-making process and all the information needed in order to keep the services of the facility important to the company.

The nonprofit sector of librarianship seems to have ignored these lessons for too many years. One questions why this may be. Perhaps it is because service-oriented librarians have traditionally believed that there will always be a need for the information provided by the library, either free or for a small cost, to anyone who needs it.

However, providing information is expensive. Materials, personnel, and facilities cost more each year. Funding is decreasing. Accountability for expenditures is a topic that now appears regularly in the literature of librarianship. Articles regularly appear on decision making in the acquisition or selection of materials. Few of these articles, however, discuss the decision-making process in terms of how the decisions are made. Instead, most of them describe the information needed or considered in the development of the decision. Certainly, knowing what information is needed as input into the process is important. Once all the data is collected, however, what does one do with it? How does a person use this information in order to make a decision?

STEPS IN THE DECISION PROCESS

In terms of collection development and selection, some conclusions can be drawn from these studies. For example, since it seems that the experienced selectors in the libraries studied have the same thought processes, using the same types of data, their thought processes can be interpreted through implementation of several of the structures outlined in the literature of administrative behavior. For this research, Mintzberg's seven routines in the decision-making process were used.[2] These routines include recognition, diagnosis, search, design, screening, evaluation/choice, and authorization. A summary of these routines, their applications to collection development, and a decision flowchart based upon these routines are presented here. (See also Figure 10.1.)

Routine 1: Recognition

The recognition routine may occur in several ways. The selector may have recognized that there is a need for greater coverage of a particular subject area in the collection. A patron or library staff member may bring to the selector's attention that a title is available and would be useful in the library. The institution in which the library operates may develop a new program, curriculum, or area of emphasis for which there are no current support materials and services offered by the library.

All selectors interviewed identified several ways by which they became aware of needs for the collections. Common to all types of libraries was the request from a patron or library staff member for a particular item or a particular subject. In all libraries studied, requests were welcomed from anyone eligible to use the library's collections and were generally purchased if funds were available.

Also common to all the libraries studied was the selector's awareness of, and knowledge of, the collections and what they contained. Selectors continually scanned favorite or appropriate reviewing sources to identify new materials that might be of interest to the community they serve. When applicable, selectors scanned bibliographies of ma-

terial in specialized subject areas and identified materials that should
be in the library's collections.

Those selectors who performed reference work were able to recognize areas in which the collections were inadequate. They used this
knowledge to select materials that would enrich the collection. They
were also able to anticipate new trends in information needs by notic-
ing patterns of questions asked by patrons.

Finally, all selectors were aware of materials in the collections that
were worn out, lost, or outdated. In most cases, replacement for such
materials was identified as a need. Often the replacement of a specific
item was desired, but occasionally a new work or new edition of an
older title was considered appropriate.

Routine 2: Diagnosis

Having recognized a need for a subject or a title within the collections, the selectors determined in all cases what characteristics would
be necessary to fulfill that need. Following criteria that had been developed over a period of time, they identified the characteristics of the
items appropriate for the collections, such as language of publication,
date of publication, date of copyright, format of material, price, and
so on.

Routine 3: Search

The search routine could occur in one of two ways. If the selector
was notified of a specific title by a requestor, the search routine consisted of checking the catalogs of the collections to determine whether
the item was already owned by the library or checking the on-order
files to see if it was on order. If the library owned or had ordered the
item, the decision-making process would be discontinued at this point.

If the need for materials was determined and no titles were brought
to the attention of the selectors, a search was instituted for items that
would fulfill the needs identified. Selectors examined the reviewing
or publishing sources in the collections to identify titles that would
fill the criteria developed in Routine 2.

Routine 4: Design

This routine involves identifying the most effective methods of acquiring the material to fulfill the needs identified earlier. An item
that would meet a short-term need might be borrowed on interlibrary
loan and the decision process ends. However, if the selector determined that the item would be of value to the collection, the design

Figure 10.1
Steps in the Decision Process

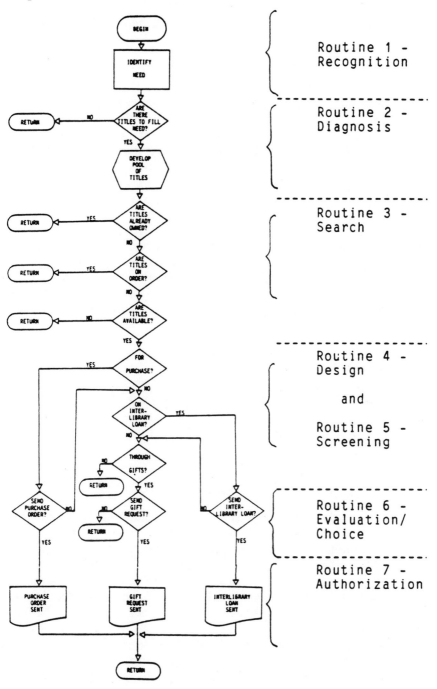

would involve determining the best method of acquiring the item, including the possibility of seeking a gift copy or purchasing it from a vendor, supplier, publisher, producer, or distributor.

Routine 5: Screening

Screening the various options for purchase is the next routine. Once the alternative sources for acquisition are determined, the selector decides which source would be the most effective in providing the material needed. Among the considerations in screening the source are accuracy and speed in fulfilling an order, supplier reputation for service, and the possibility of discounts or other monetary savings for collection budgets.

Routine 6: Evaluation/Choice

With all the information gathered in the previous routines, the selector once again evaluated whether the item should be purchased. If the item was to be purchased, the selector chose the supplier. If the item could not be borrowed on interlibrary loan or the selector decided that the item should not be purchased, the decision process cycled back to Routine 4: Design.

Routine 7: Authorization

This routine took several forms in the various libraries. Some selectors could authorize the purchase of materials only to the extent that they sent requests to a supervisor for review. Other selectors sent requests to purchasing personnel. A few of the selectors actually created and sent the orders.

STRUCTURAL LEVELS OF DISCRETION

The level of discretion allowed the selector played an important role in the decision making of all selectors. In some cases, the selectors could not complete the decision process because they were not permitted the evaluation/choice and authorization routines. Often, these were the selectors who were not aware of the outcome of their decisions. They could not state whether items they selected were actually purchased, and they did not know how much money was left in the budget for purchases.

As defined by Melcher,[3] structural levels in the formal authority relationships within an organization fall into three categories. *Extensive discretion* provides individuals with complete authority to follow the decision process to its conclusion. Such individuals can authorize actions without review. Most of the selectors with extensive discretion were administrative heads of libraries and were accountable only to the governing authority of the library.

The exception to this was the school librarian—head of the library but accountable to a media advisory committee and to the principal of the school. The school librarian was allowed *moderate discretion*, as were the majority of the selectors in these studies. Selectors with moderate discretion had their decisions reviewed by supervisors or committees. Their decisions were guided by policy and procedures, written or unwritten.

Only one of the selectors was permitted *restricted discretion*. This selector, a nonprofessional in a special library, could not make any decisions that were not approved by a supervisor. All decisions were guided by written policies, procedures, and rules for acquisition of materials.

If librarians who are given the responsibility of selecting materials for collections follow the decision process, as outlined in this work, then it seems that they, and only they, would have the background information necessary to make appropriate selections for the library's collections. It would appear that supervisors, most of whom have many other duties within the library, would not have the same amount of knowledge needed to determine the most appropriate materials and sources from which to purchase those materials. In fact, the majority of the selectors with moderate discretion felt that very few of their recommendations were rejected by their supervisors.

This raises the question of the effectiveness of providing an intermediary step in the discretionary structure of the library. If the selectors have gathered the information necessary to enable them to make a decision, and if they have followed the decision process to its conclusion, then why should their decisions be reviewed by a supervisor? Certainly, during the training process such decisions should be reviewed to ensure that the selector is following approved policies and procedures, and that the needs of the users will be met. Once training is completed, however, selectors should be granted extensive discretion to purchase materials within their areas of expertise.

With extensive discretion, there are responsibilities that must be assumed by the selector. One responsibility is that the materials selected for the collections will be appropriate to the mission, goals, and objectives of the library. The selector should be responsible for, and accountable for, collection budget expenditures, which would require timely feedback on the status of orders by the purchasing or ordering departments of the library or its institution. Selectors should also know what the library has already ordered or rejected for order, so that they may avoid duplication of effort on their own behalf and for support personnel.

Any duplication of work is counterproductive in the library environment. Therefore, it would make sense that well-trained, knowledgeable selectors should be provided with the opportunity to enhance the collections and services of the library, without unnecessary oversight. Only when patron needs are not being met by the materials in the collections should the library administration examine the effectiveness of the selector(s).

SUMMARY

Developing collections for any type of library is a task that requires commitment from the library administration. This commitment includes providing an environment within which those who select materials can use their knowledge and judgment to identify and acquire materials necessary for the provision of information and services to the community for which the library exists. It includes providing the funds necessary to purchase any needed materials and guaranteeing the availability of the funds that have been allocated, thus avoiding the problem of capital constraints. It includes the development of alternative methods of acquiring materials, such as resource-sharing agreements. The commitment also includes providing the selectors with an opportunity to follow the decision process, with few interruptions.

Selectors, too, have several responsibilities, not the least of which is to select materials that are appropriate for the collections and that meet patron needs. They must be aware of any situations that may impact the information needs of the community. Materials should be purchased in a timely fashion and should support the mission, goals, and objectives of the library. In order to accomplish this, selectors should be given extensive discretion to decide what is and what is not added to the collections. Conversely, selectors must be aware of the decision-making process. Also, they must be able to identify how their decisions are made and what information they use to make those decisions. They should periodically review their thought processes during selection of materials to be aware of any unconscious decisions.

Building library collections is not an intuitive task. It is a task that can be completed only by individuals who are well aware of the needs of the community to be served and the materials that would be appropriate to meet those needs. Experience and expertise are essential in the background of a selector, for without these it is difficult to understand the information needed in order to select materials for a library. Uninformed application of experience and expertise to collection development decision making can result in inappropriate selections, at best, and possibly even unconscious censorship.

Fortunately, the selectors in the libraries studied, while unaware of their decision processes, had experience, expertise, and a commitment to their patrons' needs. Once they became aware of their decision processes, they developed confidence that their selections were based on more than intuition; their selections were based upon relevant knowledge. Some who agreed to participate in the studies felt the need to apologize and to warn the researcher that they probably would not have much to contribute. As can be seen from this work, they had a great deal to contribute. Their unconscious decision making became conscious decision making. Conscious decision making should be the goal of every selector.

One of the most essential assets of a library is the collection that is developed to support the services offered to patrons. If the collection is inadequate or inappropriate to the mission, community, and services offered by the library, then all of these will suffer. Greater responsibility and support has to be given to those who select materials for the collections. Greater attention must be paid to the decision process by which these decisions are made. Greater emphasis should be placed on the awareness of the responsibility of the selectors to protect and promote services by acquiring adequate support materials.

Selection should not be relegated to a job duty that is done whenever there is a slow time in the library. Selectors should not have to identify titles to purchase for the collections between questions at the reference desk, or between telephone calls. Selectors should be recognized, by the entire library staff, for the essential work they do to enhance the library for the patrons, for without good selectors, who make decisions on materials based on a strong foundation of knowledge, libraries would not meet the needs of their patrons. After all, is that not what libraries were created to do?

NOTES

1. Herbert A. Simon, *Administrative Behavior: A Study of Decision-Making Process in Administrative Organization*, 3rd ed. (New York: Free Press, 1976), p. 1.

2. Henry Mintzberg, "Planning on the Left Side and Managing on the Right," *Harvard Business Review* 54 (July/August 1976): 55.

3. Arlyn J. Melcher, *Structure and Process of Organizations: A Systems Approach* (Englewood Cliffs, NJ: Prentice Hall, 1976), p. 154.

PART IV
APPENDICES

Appendix A: City "A" Public Library Policy

MATERIALS SELECTION POLICY

Purpose of the statement itself (with suggested changes):

1. To guide the library staff in the selection of materials.
2. To inform the public about the principles upon which selections are based.

Intent of the policy (with suggested changes):

1. To provide a collection of materials which will help implement the library board's overall policy and achieve its objectives. (To provide a collection of materials which will contribute to the achievement of the library board's overall policies and goals.)
2. To provide a broad collection of materials for information and research.
3. To provide materials for recreational reading. (To provide materials for recreational reading, listening, and viewing.)

4. To provide for the development of collections to meet special needs.

Responsibility

Materials selection as a privilege belongs to every member of the staff; as a responsibility it rests finally with the Director.

General Principles

1. Basic to the policy is the "Library Bill of Rights" and the "Freedom To Read Statement" of the American Library Association.

2. Selection is based on the merits of a work in relation to the needs and interests of the community and the existing book collection. (Selection is based on the merits of a work in relation to the needs and interests of the community and to the existing materials collection.)

3. Responsibility for guidance of reading by children and adolescents belongs to parents. (Responsibility for the monitoring of reading, listening and viewing choices made by children and adolescents is a responsibility of parents, not of the library.)

4. Materials containing emphasis on sex or using profanity shall not be automatically rejected without consideration of literary value. However, the selection process will exclude from library purchase those novels which are characterized by calculated eroticism in the absence of redeeming social value. (Change the word *novels* to *materials*.)

5. Selection must meet the anticipated needs of the potential user as well as the known needs of the regular user.

6. The book collection should contain opposing views on controversial topics and should represent the best possible balance among all sides of public questions.

7. The appearance of the book on a best-seller list does not in itself justify purchase.

8. The same standards for the purchase of books will be applied to gifts—no special shelves will be provided as a condition of acceptance. Exceptions will not be permitted without action of the Library Board. (The standards set in this policy will be applied to donations as well as to purchases. The library will not accept gifts of materials that do not meet the standards.

Donations will not be accepted if special conditions such as separate shelving, permanent retention, value appraisal are required by the donor. Exceptions will not be permitted by the Library Board.)

General Criteria for Selection of Materials

1. Material should meet high standards of quality in content, expression, and format.
2. The content should be authoritative and significant.
3. Materials should have either current interest, permanent value, or both.
4. It should be significant in comparison with other material on the same subject.
5. It should have received some favorable critical attention.
6. The physical book should be of sufficient quality to withstand library use.

Appendix B: City "B" Public Library Policy

COLLECTION DEVELOPMENT ACTIVITIES FOR U.S. DOCUMENTS

I. Audience
   A. Business and professional people who use the documents for work-related and personal projects and questions
   B. Adult members of the general public who use the documents for work-related and personal projects and questions
   C. Young adult and some undergraduate college students who use the collection for course-related research
II. Currency of materials
   A. Almost all materials acquired will be those currently listed in U.S. government document selection sources
   B. Exceptions will be made in cases of replacement of important lost titles
III. Coverage
   A. Reference items acquired will cover
      1. Basic documents such as the *Statistical Abstract of the United States* and the *Zip Code Directory*

   2. Broader references for a library of moderate size such as the *Economic Report of the President*, the *Dictionary of Occupational Titles*, and selected census reports

   3. Supporting references such as selected documents dealing with the state or the local history collection, selected economic census reports for the business collection, and selected documents dealing with the handicapped and services to them for the handicapped materials collection

  B. Circulating items acquired will cover

   1. Selected documents on topics of perennial interest such as drugs and smoking and health

   2. Selected documents from popular categories such as country studies (formerly area handbooks) and various NASA publications

   3. Selected documents on topics of current interest such as "star wars" space weapons and acid rain

   4. Selected documents on how-to topics such as computer programming, home improvement, diving, etc.

  C. Periodicals acquired will cover

   1. Basics such as the *Congressional Record* and *Federal Register*

   2. Statistics such as *Economic Indicators* and *Monthly Labor Review*

   3. Support (supporting special collections) such as *Commerce Business Daily* (for business collection) and *Disabled USA* (for handicapped materials collection)

IV. Selection sources

  A. *Publications Reference File*

  B. *New Books*

  C. *U.S. Government Books*

  D. *Monthly Catalog*

  E. *Consumer Information Catalog*

  F. Agency lists

  G. *Booklist*

  H. Media of all types

  I. Suggestions from the staff and the public

  J. *Vertical File Index*

Appendix C: County Public Library Policy

This is the only library resource and information center that serves all the people of the county. The county also has a number of college, school, and special libraries. Highly technical and scholarly collections remain the responsibility of those special libraries.

It is the responsibility of the County Public Library to select, organize, and make available information, research and recreational materials. In its activities, the system will emphasize educational and informational pursuits above recreational ones. Books, periodicals, pamphlets, maps, 16mm and 8mm films, filmstrips, records, tapes, and framed art prints, among other items, are all considered appropriate library materials.

The library strives to reach all age groups in the community and recognizes specific responsibilities for each group. Of primary concern is the out of school adult who has no ready access to other library collections. A responsibility to provide initial experience with library materials to pre-school children, also to whom no other library is available, is recognized. Finally, the library strives to provide materials for the reading and reference needs of the county's student population, supplementing resources available in the school and college libraries. The library will cooperate with other civic and cultural organizations in the community and will support with its resources their program objectives. The library has a special responsibility to serve as an information resource for all government agencies operating in the county.

RESPONSIBILITY FOR SELECTION

The ultimate responsibility for selection rests with the director of the library, who operates within the framework of policies recommended by the Library Board and ratified by the Board of County Commissioners. Initial selection, however, can be delegated by the director to various professional staff members by reason of position and training.

INTELLECTUAL FREEDOM

The library subscribes to the book selecting principles contained in the "Library Bill of Rights" and "Freedom To Read Statement" adopted by the American Library Association.

CRITERIA FOR SELECTION

Within standards of purpose and quality, library materials are selected to meet the cultural, informational, and recreational needs and interests of the community. Materials are added when they are of current and potential value to individuals and groups with varying levels of interest, age, and ability. The library will always be guided by a sense of responsibility to both present and future users in adding materials which enrich the collection and maintain overall balance.

All material, whether purchased or donated, are considered in terms of the following standards:

- authority and competence in presentation
- authority and competence in content
- aesthetic and literary value
- current or historical significance
- potential or known use by patrons
- importance to total collection
- appearance of the title in important bibliographies, lists, or recognized reviewing media
- timeliness and/or current value
- scarcity of materials elsewhere in subject area

- price
- appropriateness of format to content

An item, however, need not meet *all* of the criteria in order to be acceptable. Books and other materials will be considered as whole works and may not be excluded on the basis of individual passages taken out of context.

CONTROVERSIAL SUBJECTS

The following subject fields need further explanation:

Human Reproduction and Sexual Behavior

The library is responsible for providing authoritative, scientifically accurate, up-to-date, unsensational [*sic*] materials on sex. Materials appropriate for various age and interest levels will be acquired. Books concerning sexual deviation or the morbid, perverse conditions of society are bought only to the extent that they give insight into the problems. In the selection of any book in this area, judgment is based on the total work, rather than words, phrases, or situations, which in themselves may be objectional [*sic*].

Religion

The library recognizes an obligation to provide materials about the major denominations, especially those represented locally. It also includes information about the beliefs, practices, and rituals of many sects, if presented with authority, accuracy, and objectivity. In addition to materials pertaining to individual beliefs, the collection contains basic authoritative studies in the areas of history of religion, theology, comparative religion, and mythology. The collection also encompasses popular studies on new trends, ideas, and movements that are currently taking place in the field of religion.

Politics and Campaign Literature

The library recognizes a particular responsibility to provide material representing all points of view concerning political issues. However, the library does not purchase or accept for dissemination slanted campaign literature for a particular candidate's background and platform.

PERIODICALS, NEWSPAPERS, MICROFORM

Periodicals are purchased to keep the library collection up-to-date on current issues, to provide material not yet in book form, for reference work, and general reading.

Representative newspapers of leading cities across the country, as well as a comprehensive collection of area and state newspapers, are selected.

Back issues of selected newspapers, as well as other records requiring much space for storage, are purchased in microform. This enables the library to retain material that would otherwise be discarded because of space requirements or deterioration.

AUDIOVISUAL MATERIALS

The library recognizes the cultural, educational, and aesthetic impact of audiovisual media on the public, and, therefore, maintains a well-rounded collection of nonprint materials to complete the library's total media collection. Sixteen millimeter films are selected for their cultural, educational, and recreational value to community groups. Strictly instructional curriculum-oriented films are avoided for the most part since these films are available through the school system. Filmstrips, framed art prints, and phonograph records fill out the audiovisual materials collection.

SPECIAL COLLECTIONS

State and Local History and Genealogy

The Local History Room collection will acquire, within limitations of budget and facilities, materials that reflect the political, social, cultural, and economic life of the county, state, and region of the United States. Standards for the general collection may not always apply, since inclusiveness is the goal in regard to materials produced in and about the county.

A limited amount of genealogical materials will be acquired, the majority dealing with the state, some with the region, still fewer of a general nature. The library will cooperate, as far as possible, with groups and individuals interested in local history.

Government Documents

For several decades, the main library has been a limited depository for selected U.S. government documents. Publications in chosen series are received free from the U.S. Government Printing Office. The library also purchases useful documents not received on depository and duplicates depository items as needed.

GIFTS, DUPLICATION, RESERVES, AND WITHDRAWALS

Gifts

Books and related materials: The library welcomes gifts of books and other related materials with the understanding that these will be evaluated in accordance with the criteria for selection stated earlier. The library reserves the right to keep or dispose of any material that may be donated.

The system will accept as many as three religious books per library from any one denomination on strictly doctrinal subjects, if these books meet the criteria for selection. The library reserves the right to withdraw them on the same basis as other library material.

Money: Gifts of money for the purchase of books and other materials are welcome. The library appreciates flexibility in the use of the donation for the enrichment of the collection.

Appraisal of gifts: The library will give a monetary appraisal of gifts for the donor's tax purposes, if the request is made at the time of the donation.

Memorials: The library encourages the giving of cash donations or books as memorials. The donor may designate a particular subject field or title. The library will send an acknowledgment of the memorial to the donor and an announcement of the donation to the family of the person memorialized.

Duplication

The library attempts to weigh the specific demand in relation to the total library program and policies. Materials that are in great demand and selected titles on current problems may be duplicated. Paperbacks and rental collection books may be used to supplement further demand.

Reserves

Any materials in the collection may be reserved. Duplication is considered on the basis of accumulated reserves.

Withdrawals

Replacement: The library's policy is to consider for replacement all books withdrawn because of loss, damage, or wear. Replacement in each case is based on the following factors: adequate coverage in the field by later and better material and demand for the specific title.

Weeding of books and other materials: Weeding is a thorough and conscientious effort to achieve a well-balanced collection suitable to the patrons served and should be a continuous, consistent process. Books and other materials that are obsolete, soiled, damaged, or no longer useful in the light of the selection standards or purposes of the library shall be systematically removed from the collection. In some instances an irreplaceable title of importance must be retained regardless of condition. Special handling will be given to such titles.

MAIN AND BRANCH COLLECTIONS

The branches will concentrate on popular and current materials and will rely upon main collection to supply in-depth information and retrospective materials.

Since the various units serve people with a wide range of interests, each unit will select materials with its individual clientele in mind. In making their selections, branch librarians will not be limited to those materials that are in the Main Library.

(Adopted by the Board of Trustees: August 1974.)

Appendix D: Two-County Regional Public Library Policy

SELECTION OF LIBRARY MATERIALS

On an annual basis each library receives a set percentage of the total materials budget for the system. The percentage is based on circulation and number of patrons. Library personnel responsible for book selection should forward selection journals to their supervisor for weekly book selection meetings at the main library. In addition to selection journals and best-seller lists, materials are considered for purchase when the library has received two patron requests from the community.

The general guidelines for book selection are further outlined in the materials selection policy that follows.

A lease plan through a large wholesaler has been established for each library to be able to provide an adequate supply of popular adult books for its patrons. Each library handles its own plan, and appropriate branch personnel and the head of circulation and main librarian are responsible for selecting, ordering, and returning lease books.

MATERIALS SELECTION POLICY

Purpose

The library undertakes as its primary responsibility to provide the best possible public library service to meet the varied needs and interests of county residents. This materials selection policy is designed to aid the library to serve this community in terms of tastes, habits, attitudes, and interests of the people. Materials are selected in accordance with the ALA "Library Bill of Rights" and the ALA "Freedom To Read Statement." Its primary objective is to insure that public monies are spent wisely so that the library can provide the community with relevant materials in sufficient supply to make the library a dependable resource for most people most of the time.

Responsibility for Selection of Materials

The Board of Trustees has ultimate legal authority for all selection at the library. While appropriate members of the library staff participate in reviewing and evaluating library materials for purchase, the final responsibility for selection is delegated to the director, who operates within the guidelines set by the Board of Trustees.

Definitions

Selection refers to the decision that must be made either to add a specific item or type of material to the collection or to retain material already in the collection. It is a means of collection development to meet user needs and does not necessarily reflect the opinions or values of the individual selector or of the Library Board.

The words *book*, *library materials*, and other synonyms as they may appear in this policy have the widest possible meaning; all forms of recorded communication, from the traditional printed forms to the latest development in nonprofit media, are therefore included in this definition.

The word *collection* refers to a group of books or other library material having a common characteristic or located in one place.

Organization of the Library as a Factor in Selection

The library is composed of facilities and collections that are designed to make its total resources readily available and widely accessible to the community it serves. The regional system presently includes: the main library with extensive reference resources, departmental and special collections, and comprehensive adult and children's circulating collections; branch libraries in six cities that have collections of general reading and reference materials planned to meet the particular needs of their communities.

' Because the needs of the users of the individual units vary, so must the collections chosen for them, and it is in this respect that the organization of the library affects the selection of materials.

Criteria for Selection and Evaluation of Materials

1. authority and reputation of the author (training, field of specialization, contributions)
2. content of the book (objectivity, accuracy or distortion of ideas)
3. style (clarity, readability, manner of presentation)
4. format of publication
5. value (permanent, current, temporary, educational, recreational)
6. popular demand
7. evaluation of critical reviewers
8. reputation of the publisher
9. books owned by the library that treat the same subject
10. common sense

Use of the Library's Collection

The library recognizes that many books are controversial and that any given item may offend some patrons. Selections will not be made on the basis of any assumed approval or disapproval, but solely on the merit of the work as it relates to the library's objectives and serves the expressed or anticipated needs and interests of the community.

Responsibility for the reading of minors rests with their parents and legal guardians. Selection of adult materials will not be limited by the possibility that books may come into the possession of minors.

Gifts and Donations

The library accepts gifts with the understanding that they will not necessarily be added to the library's collection. The material will be judged by the same standards of selection as those applied to the purchase of new materials. If the materials are not suitable because of condition, outdated information, or other factors, they will be referred to other institutions, sold, or discarded. The library does not appraise gifts.

Books and other materials may be donated at any time throughout the year. All donations should be accepted only after the staff member has explained the terms under which donations are accepted. Upon request, a statement of the number of items donated will be supplied; however, the library cannot give a cost evaluation of the donation. If requested by the donor, the staff member receiving the materials should fill out the tax donation form that is kept at all circulation desks and the Technical Services Department at the main library.

Donated materials should be sent as soon as possible to the Technical Services Department at the main library. Materials are then placed in one designated area for checking by the head of extension or the librarian for the main library. Materials needed for inclusion in the main library or branch collections are then processed according to established procedures. Materials not needed by any library are then used for upcoming book sales, given to another institution, or discarded.

Re-evaluation of the Collection

Systematic removal from the collection of material no longer useful is essential to maintaining the purposes and quality of resources. The discarding of materials requires the same degree of attention as initial selection and deserves careful study.

Weeding is an integral part of book selection by which a library removes worn, outdated, and unused books from its shelves. Systematic weeding is not an irresponsible disposal of public property, but a public service that is often the most needed act in increasing library use. A smaller collection that is good, viable, attractive, and used is a greater credit to a community than a large number of books that tend to remain on the shelves because of poor format or poor content. Weeding will be done by qualified library personnel based on the following considerations:

1. worn out through use
2. ephemeral material that is no longer timely
3. books no longer considered accurate or factual
4. combination of little use and questionable value
5. excess copies of a title no longer in demand

It is the library's policy not to replace automatically all books withdrawn. Need for replacement is considered in relation to the following:

1. number of duplicate copies
2. existence of adequate coverage in the collection
3. demand for specific title or subject
4. the value of the individual title, whether for literary quality, subject appeal, or authority and importance of the author
5. availability of newer and better materials in the field

Appendix E: City Public Schools Policy

SELECTION OF INSTRUCTIONAL MATERIALS

Definition of Instructional Materials: Basic and supplemental textbooks, media center materials, and any other type of print or nonprint media used in the classroom and/or media center to implement the instructional program in grades K–12.

Philosophy

The responsibility of the personnel of the public schools is to provide for all students the instructional materials, print and nonprint, that will best serve to prepare the students for the kind of meaningful and productive place in society that each individual deserves. In order to achieve this task, it is necessary to select materials that will present a wide range of ideas and information to insure against the projection of biased or limited views of life. Democracy rests on the assumption that the educated, free person can be entrusted with self-determination. It should be recognized, however, that not every student has achieved the same level of intellectual ability or maturity; therefore, the professional staff is charged with the duty of assisting and advising the student in selecting and using those materials that will best serve individual needs.

Objectives

1. Provide materials to enrich and support the curriculum, taking into consideration the varied interests, abilities and maturity levels of the pupils served.
2. Provide materials to stimulate growth in factual knowledge, literary appreciation, aesthetic values and ethical standards.
3. Provide a background of information to enable pupils to make intelligent judgments and to sharpen their critical evaluation skills.
4. Provide pro and con materials on controversial issues so that young citizens may develop the practice of critical analysis of all media.
5. Provide materials representative of the diversity of our American heritage.
6. Place principle above personal opinion and reason above prejudice in the selection of materials of the highest quality to assure a comprehensive collection appropriate for the users.
7. Provide materials that develop a positive image of men and women free of sexual bias.

Hierarchy of Responsibility

1. superintendent
2. area assistant superintendent
3. principal
4. system-wide director/assistant director
5. librarian
6. media advisory committee
7. teacher

Selection Processes, Procedures, and Principles

I. Responsibility for the evaluation of instructional materials is shared jointly by members of the staff, members of the Media Advisory Committee, and the media specialist (librarian). Instructional materials purchased with any school funds (local, state, federal, personal, PTA, etc.) must have the approval of the Media Advisory Committee and the principal prior to utilization in the classroom and/or media center. While it is not practical to require that every textbook or library book be read word for word, it is the responsibility of the Media Advisory Committee and the principal to be sure that books, both fiction and nonfiction, are read sufficiently to be properly evaluated.

II. Evaluation of materials is a continuous process with adequate time provided for the following:
A. Examination, previewing, or field testing
B. Reference to reviews
C. Reference to reputable, unbiased, professionally prepared selection aids

III. Suggestions and/or requests are submitted to the Media Advisory Committee through the media specialists (librarians).

IV. The Media Advisory Committee and subcommittees will analyze print and nonprint materials and evaluate them critically using the objectives listed in Section II and the following additional criteria:
A. Authenticity and/or historical perspective
B. Reputation and significance of author/artist/composer/producer
C. Relationship to the curriculum and the collection
D. Technical quality
E. Cost

V. Free and/or donated materials and donated funds for instructional materials are accepted if:
A. Materials meet the same criteria and evaluation that are used with the purchased materials.
B. The Media Advisory Committee will recommend to the principal what instructional materials will be purchased with donated funds and what free materials will be accepted for use in the school.

Utilization

1. Instructional materials are organized for quick, easy, and equal access to all students and teachers in the individual school.

2. The superintendent has the authority to direct the redistribution of instructional materials among individual schools in order to insure that instructional materials are utilized to the maximum extent.

Personal Benefits from Vendors

No employee of the public schools shall receive any type of personal gift, materials, free meals, or financial remuneration from a book salesperson during a textbook adoption year or from a vendor whose instructional materials are in the process of being formally evaluated for use within the school system. All vendors receive fair and equitable treatment in the purchase process.

(For weeding and discarding, the policies of the State Department of Education, Appendix G, follow.)
Approved: Summer 1980.

Appendix F: County Public Schools Policy

SELECTION OF INSTRUCTIONAL MATERIALS

Policy

The Board of Education recognizes the importance of using a wide variety of instructional materials, equipment, and activities, in addition to adopted textbooks, to assist teachers in meeting the instructional needs of students. Further, the Board believes that the standards for selection, evaluation, and funding of instructional materials must be uniform systemwide. These standards must reflect the responsibility of public education to meet the wide variety of learning needs throughout the system.

The Board of Education directs the superintendent and/or his designee to establish the standards and procedures for the selection process.

Procedure

Selection of instructional materials shall be an on-going procedure. In order to more adequately ensure the appropriateness of the instructional materials to the program, it shall be the responsibility of the principal to involve the appropriate person(s) from the various program areas. These persons will review and evaluate potential materials using selection and evaluation criteria listed below before submitting their requests to the principal of the school.

The superintendent and/or his designee may serve as an advisor in the selection process. The principal will review the requests and make final decisions.

All schools shall centralize their instructional materials and equipment so that the materials may be accessible to more teachers and students.

In selecting instructional materials, the following criteria will serve as a guide:

Materials or equipment

1. that can fulfill an identified need in the curriculum;

2. that are appropriate to the curriculum;

3. that stimulate growth in factual knowledge, specific physical or mental skills, literary appreciation, ethical standards, critical thinking, aesthetic values, and problem solving;

4. that consider the individual needs, interests, abilities, socioeconomic backgrounds and maturity levels of students;

5. that present opposing sides of controversial issues so that students, under guidance, may develop and practice critical thinking and analysis;

6. that represent the many religious, ethnic, and cultural groups in our nation and the contributions of these groups to our American heritage;

7. that are based on principle rather than opinion, and reason rather than prejudice in order to assure a comprehensive collection of instructional materials;

8. appropriate for the level of students who will have access to them;

9. that have a historical perspective, and are authentic and reliable;

10. whose author, artist, composer and/or producer holds a reputation of significance;

11. that have definable educational or social value and will not be disruptive to the educational process;

12. that have good technical qualities; and

13. whose initial cost or maintenance cost is in proportion to needs and priorities in schools' plans.

Free and donated materials and donated funds for instructional materials can be accepted if the materials or equipment meet the same selection and evaluation criteria that are used with purchased materials.

(For weeding and discarding, the policies of the State Department of Education, Appendix G, follow.)
Approved: Summer 1985.

Appendix G: State Department of Education Policy

MAINTAINING A QUALITY MEDIA COLLECTION THROUGH SYSTEMATIC WEEDING

A prerequisite for maintaining a quality, up-to-date collection of media is a thorough and complete evaluation of all materials and equipment in the collection. Weeding the school media collection by discarding materials and removing equipment no longer useful is a task as important as selecting new media of high quality. Although state, regional, and national media guidelines may define a minimum quantity of materials and equipment that should be included in schools, the quantities stipulated are intended to refer only to quality media.

Materials

Worn and obsolete materials discourage students in their search for reliable information, encourage users to handle materials carelessly, and detract from the appearance of the school media collection. The best service from the school media program is given when the materials are up-to-date and in good condition. Users should be able to rely upon the materials as being the best available.

The entire collection should be examined at least once a year to identify those materials that need to be discarded. The practice of continuously weeding materials throughout the year may be the most manageable, the most effective, and the least disruptive of services to students and teachers. At no time should the school's media center be closed for weeding or inventory.

A written policy stating procedures for maintenance of a quality media collection should be developed for the school system under the leadership of professional media personnel and should be formally adopted by the local Board of Education. The policy should contain criteria for evaluating and weeding the collection and should state characteristics identifying materials to be permanently discarded. Such characteristics would include, but are not necessarily limited to, the following:

- poor physical condition (yellowed, brittle, scratched, warped, torn, or otherwise marred for use)
- outdated format (fine print, unattractive visuals)
- obsolete and/or inaccurate content
- inappropriate subject or treatment of the subject when considered in relation to the needs of the users
- mediocre or poor quality presentation of content (consider literary, audio, and visual qualities)

Media whose contents are partially outdated should be considered totally outdated. All materials weeded from the collection should be permanently discarded unless they can be returned for credit on new materials. (Materials that can be traded include 16mm films, filmstrips, etc.) Procedures for disposal of weeded materials should be clearly established and followed.

Some suggested procedures for weeding and discarding materials are:

1. Work with a manageable group of materials and records at a time.
2. Remove and keep in order the materials to be discarded from the collection.
3. Write in pencil on the shelflist card for each item being discarded the word *Discard* and the date (month, year). Remove the card from the shelflist unless a duplicate remains in the collection. If a duplicate remains in the collection, write the word *Discard* and the date on the shelflist card by the copy

number of the item being discarded, and leave the card in the shelflist.

4. Keep in order the cards removed from the shelflist. These cards will be used later as guides to removing the author, title, and subject cards from the card catalog. They will also be used to give a correct inventory record.

5. Keep, by type of material and category, a running count of the items being discarded for which the shelflist cards continue to remain in the shelflist.

6. Stamp the materials *Discard*. All materials weeded from the collection are permanently discarded (or traded in for discounts) according to the policy approved by the local Board of Education.

7. Itemize and record number(s) of media discarded on appropriate inventory reports.

Equipment

It is important that each school media program provide for the systematic evaluation and weeding of instructional equipment as well as materials. Since the instructional equipment should be kept in operative condition through preventive maintenance and repair, the equipment that should be weeded from the collection is that which:

- is beyond repair or is financially impractical to repair
- has outlived its usefulness
- is replaced by more effective and/or convenient equipment

Some used equipment can be traded in for discounts on the price of new equipment or can be sold outright by the Division of Purchase and Contract in the State Department of Administration. The copy of the current state contract for audiovisual equipment, sent annually to the superintendent of each school system, should be consulted for specific information. Procedures for the disposal of equipment withdrawn from school collections should be clearly defined by the local administrative unit.

The date (month, year) and the method of disposal used should be written on the inventory control card for each item of equipment that is withdrawn. This information should be recorded also on any duplicate copies of the inventory control card that may be kept in other locations (e.g., in the system-level equipment repair center). Remove the card from the current inventory list and place it with cards or other withdrawn equipment. Retain these cards until the information on them is no longer needed to substantiate inventory and financial reports.

(Issued September 1975)

Appendix H: Parochial School Policy

PHILOSOPHY

Each school should have a written statement of the church's philosophy regarding general objectives for school library media center services. Generally, these statements affirm the American freedoms contained in the *Library Bill of Rights*, the *School Library Bill of Rights*, and the *Student's Right to Read*.

School library media center collections should meet the requirements of various curricular areas and provide for each individual according to his learning ability. Materials available should inspire the student, meet his individual needs, and offer depth in research. They should significantly help a student to develop a balanced cultural life and to learn to be a free, reasoning person. Of high quality and broad dimension, materials should enable a student to take advantage of current technology.

The collection should reflect current trends in education and communication. The findings of research in learning development, increased sophistication of youth, rising expectations of deprived children, the crisis of ghetto and/or central city should influence the selection and use of materials.

Materials selection is the responsibility of qualified specialists at the local, state, regional, or national levels. The process of selection is expedited by consulting reviews, recommended lists, standard bibliographic tools, and special releases.

SUGGESTED GOALS FOR SCHOOL LIBRARY MEDIA CENTERS

An effective school library media center should:

- support instruction in all areas of curriculum, with a richness of materials made easily accessible
- increase opportunity for self-directed learning for lifelong education and enjoyment
- develop appreciation of our cultural heritage and responsibilities of citizenship
- improve and extend educational opportunities for pupils of all racial and ethnic backgrounds
- encourage innovative ways of teaching learning through the use of instructional media
- involve members of the community and enlist their support
- maintain supportive staff in sufficient number qualified to implement diverse services
- provide an environment conducive to learning

MATERIALS SELECTION POLICY

The selection of library books is the particular responsibility of the librarian with the approval of the principal under authorization from the Board of Education. All requests are evaluated by the librarian on the basis of the "Policies of Selection," and if there are any questions as to the suitability of the material for the school library, a review copy should be obtained and examined personally by the librarian and the persons making the request. Generally recognized and accepted reviewing media are used to check and evaluate requests for materials, and wherever possible the librarian should examine the book itself in depositories, shops, and publishers' exhibits prior to purchase.

Each year the collection should be thoroughly examined to determine the various subject areas that need strengthening in order to fulfill the purpose of the library media center program. Suggestions from teachers, supervisors, students, and parents are invited and welcomed, but the final decision is made by the librarian. Criteria for his/her choice are *quality* as determined by standard reviewing services and bibliographies, and subjective weighing of curriculum needs in the individual school with assignment of priorities on that basis. A curriculum change of any proportion necessitates priority for material in that field. The librarian makes the final choices *after* checking standard tools and guides.

Suggestions are then given intending to help build quality while adding quantity in the following areas: content, format, price, suitability, and other considerations for reference materials. Magazines and audiovisual materials are also addressed.

DISCARDING

Weeding is second in importance to selection. Both print and nonprint materials must be weeded.
What materials should I discard?

1. materials that are worn, or damaged beyond mending or rebinding
2. materials whose pages are yellow, brittle, soiled, loose, or disfigured
3. materials replaced by new or revised editions, by more up-to-date titles, by a more sophisticated format, or by more comprehensive works
4. materials that are inaccurate, misleading, and out-of-date
5. materials that are mediocre, that is, they do not inform the reader or provide high literary merit
6. books with very fine print
7. books that do not circulate more than once or twice in three years

How do I clear the records and discard materials?

1. Tear out the card and pocket.
2. Pull all the cards from the main catalog.
3. Cross off accessions book and mark *discarded* and year.
4. Take materials completely out of media center facility.
5. Destroy by putting them in school dumpster.
6. Clip sparingly for possible vertical file or picture file usage.
7. Tear off the back, tear down the spine, and use for paper drive.

Guidelines for discarding nonfiction:

000   *Encyclopedias*: New edition is needed at least every
           five years.

           Bibliographies: Seldom of use after 10 years from date
           of copyright.

100   *Ethics, etc.*: Value determined by use. Adjust to leave
           popular topics such as curiosities and wonders.

200   *Religion*: Collection should contain basic information
           (but not propaganda) about as many sects and reli-
           gions as possible.

300   *Social Sciences*: See that all subjects in this field are
           well represented.

           • 310 *Almanacs and Yearbooks*: Superseded by each
             new volume. Seldom of much use after five years.

           • 320 *Politics and Economics*: Books dealing with his-
             torical aspects determined by use. Discard after ap-
             proximately 10 years. Replace with new editions
             when available.

           • 340 *Government*: 10 years. Watch for new material
             on government to supersede older.

400   *Languages*: Keep basic material; weeding depends on
           use.

500   *Pure Science*: Except for botany and natural history,
           science books are usually out of date within five years
           or less. Try to keep collection current by discarding
           and purchase.

600–618   *Inventions, Medicine*: Five years, except for basic ma-
           terial on inventions and anatomy.

           • 620 *Applied Science*: Five years unless book con-
             tains material of historic value.

           • 621 *Radio, Television*: Five years at most; progress-
             ing too rapidly to be of use longer unless describing
             crystal set or other subject in demand for historical
             reference.

           • 630 *Farms, Gardens, etc.*: Keep up-to-date with new
             editions and new material to replace older.

           • 640 *Home Economics*: According to use. Keep mostly
             current material.

- 650 *Business, etc.*: 10 years.

- 660 *Chemical, Food Products*: 5 to 10 years, according to content.

- 690 *Manufacturing, Building*: 10 years, except that older books on crafts, clocks, toys may be useful.

700   *Art, Music*: Keep basic material.

800   *Literature*: Keep basic material. Keep an eye to the current favorites needed for term papers and other references.

900   *History*: Depends on use and needs of school program and on accuracy of fact and fairness of interpretation. Remove works on countries whose names and governments have undergone drastic changes.

Appendix I: College "B" Library Policy

INTRODUCTION

The Library and Its Setting

College "B" is established as a four-year interdenominational, coeducational, evangelical, bible college. The college is committed to providing a strong Christian education in biblical, professional and general studies. It provides the highest possible quality education for the individual development of each student.

The primary mission of the library is to support the curriculum of College "B." The development of the collection should reflect the current offerings and be able to expand with the natural evolution of the programs. The library should also strive to provide the faculty with the necessary resources for continual research needed for the present and evolving curriculum. Last, the library should also be a center of biblical, theological and Christian educational materials made available to pastors, church leaders, and interested lay people of the community.

The Library's Clientele

First and foremost, the library is a learning facility made available for student and faculty use. Our primary goal is to provide adequate research and curriculum-support materials for our immediate college community.

The community-at-large may also benefit from the library's collection. Pastors, church leaders, and lay people of the community are welcome to use the facility and materials to assist in their on-going ministry.

The Library's Organization

At the present time the library staff includes: director of library services, associate librarian, assistant librarian, and student assistants.

The Library's Committee

The Library Committee is a major standing committee of the faculty serving in an advisory capacity. It should convey an awareness of the users' concerns, perceptions, and needs to the library and an understanding of the library's objectives and capabilities to the users. The committee may assist in evaluation and long-range planning of the facilities and resources. Finally it should encourage faculty involvement in the selection and use of library materials.

Composition of the Library Committee should include representatives of the various academic divisions, an administrative representative, student representative with the director of library services as chair. The academic dean may also serve as an ex-officio member.

SELECTION

Selection Responsibility

Faculty members, division heads, staff, and administration are encouraged to make recommendations for materials. These recommendations are submitted to the director of library services. The director of library services and/or a professional staff member assigned this responsibility determines if

1. The book is already in the collection
2. The book is available
3. The book falls within the selection criteria for the library

If the material falls within the selection criteria and is not already owned by the library it will be placed in the material request file.

The ultimate responsibility for the quality and balance of the collection rests with the professional library staff, and they are in the best position to maintain these aspects. Subsequently, the final decision for selection and purchase of new materials for all subject areas will be made by the director of library services and/or the professional staff.

Selection Criteria

In selecting and acquiring material, the following criteria will be considered:

1. *Scope.* Primary attention will be given to the support of the curriculum of College "B." Since the college offers general education classes as well as specialized study, effort will be made to provide adequate support for this general area of human knowledge. Materials unrelated to the curriculum in general, cultural, or religious areas are available in limited quantities. Collection and addition of these materials is dependent upon donations and available space. It is not the intention of the library to compete with local public libraries in collecting material of a recreational nature.

2. *Value.* The selection process shall give major consideration to the authority, accuracy, timeliness, and reputation of the author and publisher. Evaluation of the material's importance shall be based on reviews, bibliographies, and/or the professional judgment of the faculty and librarians.

3. *Format.* The library may collect and preserve materials in any type of format that can be adapted to or used by the present facilities of the library. This includes print, cassettes, videotapes, manuscripts, microforms, slides, filmstrips, computer software, and other audiovisuals.

4. *Duplication.* In most cases, only one copy of an item will be purchased. Faculty needing multiple copies for reserve or special class material should submit a special request for these duplications to the director of library services for consideration.

5. *Categories of Materials Not Acquired*:
    (a). Materials that are excessively priced, particularly rare, out-of-print, antiquarian books
    (b). Textbooks of a general survey nature, published for

classroom use. Exception—elementary education tests will be collected and limited quantities may be purchased. Donations from publishers should be pursued for this type of material

(c). Foreign language materials for which neither faculty nor students have reading skills

(d). Materials of recreational nature typically collected by a public library

Selection Levels

The library will select and collect materials on three levels. Materials that do not directly support the curriculum will be collected from the minimal to basic range. Minimal provides for specific reference works or one or two well-known classics. Basic provides for materials that introduce and generally define the subject. This allows the library to have a broad selection of cultural and religious materials, thereby offering a balanced collection.

Curricular support materials will be collected in the range of initial to advanced study. This range provides for support of the course work with emphasis on the undergraduate level. Broadening to advanced provides some graduate level material for faculty research.

Selection of Serials and Indexes

Serials are purchased, or gift subscriptions are accepted, for the following reasons

1. To provide current information in various fields of study
2. To provide information not available in any other format
3. To offer current scholarship for faculty in the various fields of study
4. To aid in material selection
5. To provide current news items, religious current events, and cultural exposure

Suggestions for new serial subscriptions need to be submitted by March of each year. At this point, an evaluation of serial holdings and subscriptions will be made. Additions or deletions will be determined by the following criteria

1. Support by the serial for the college curriculum
2. Number of serials supporting the given field

3. Accuracy and objectivity of the serial

4. Accessibility of the serial through indexes

5. Cost of the subscription in relation to its use

Subscriptions targeted for deletion will be discussed with the appropriate division head. If the serial is found to be essential, it will be reconsidered and alternative funding methods may be sought.

COLLECTION MAINTENANCE

Evaluation

A growing library collection requires systematic and periodic evaluation. There are three approaches to evaluation that will be considered. The first deals with direct support for the college curriculum. Course offerings have been assigned general classification designations. This allows a fairly quick overview as to whether material falls into one of these designated areas.

The second approach requires the use of checking holdings against specialized bibliographies.

The final approach relies on faculty expertise for a given subject field. Material that does not fall into at least one of the three checklists could be listed as questionable for the collection.

Deselection

Books targeted by evaluation, lack of space, aging materials, and those unable to be repaired may fall into the category for deselection. Materials may be designated for deselection by the professional library staff or faculty members. Materials targeted for deselection by faculty members must be reviewed by the division head. The final decision for deselection, however, rests with the director of library services. Possible criteria for deselection:

1. Do we own a later edition or superior revision?

2. Is the material outdated by later works?

3. Is it relevant to the present curriculum?

4. Will it contribute to the evolving curriculum?

5. Is it a duplicate? Are multiple copies necessary?

6. Is the material in need of repair/beyond repair?

7. Has the material circulated in five to ten years?

Inventory

A systematic inventory should be done of the collection over a two-year period. Missing materials should be identified and their records removed. These records should be held for one year, after which they are discarded if the item is not found.

Replacement

It is not an automatic policy to replace items withdrawn because of loss, damage, or wear. Several factors are considered

1. Number of duplicate copies
2. Coverage of subject area is adequate
3. Materials of later or better quality owned
4. Demand for use shown in circulation records
5. Availability of the item

Conservation and Preservation

Conservation and preservation are topics that are not often considered in a collection development policy. They are, however, essential to the overall maintenance of the collection.

Careful consideration should be given to the type of format for materials selected, particularly in the case of print. Will the item withstand the expected use in its original format? Should paperbacks be purchased when hardcover is available? Should certain materials automatically be scheduled to be rebound?

GIFTS

Policies for Gifts of Materials

The library is frequently offered books and other library materials. In order to avoid confusion or misunderstanding, the library has established specific criteria for gifts of materials.

1. The director of library services and/or professional staff shall reserve the right to refuse gift materials that do not fall within the selection criteria or will not contribute to the mission of the library.

2. If materials are accepted for consideration, the donor should be aware that

   (a) The professional staff shall determine the classification, housing, and circulating policies for all gift items

   (b) The library reserves the right to dispose of duplicate or unneeded materials as it sees fit

   (c) Gifts will be acknowledged with a letter from the college administration but will not include tax evaluation

Policies for Gifts of Funds

A library's book budget is always limited in light of the rising publishing costs. Outside funds are a way to supplement book budgets. The library welcomes donations with the following criteria:

1. The director of library services and/or professional staff shall reserve the right for the disposition of these funds

2. Donations, with strict or limiting restrictions that do not fall within the collection development policy, may be refused

3. Donors wishing to limit or restrict funds may be asked to reconsider or select some other area for their donation if their restrictions do not fall within the collection development policy

Special Collections

Due to limitations of space and personnel, gifts of material that would require special handling or constitute a special collection must be considered by the director of library services and the Library Committee. If the special collection would be a substantial addition, the college administration may be asked to make provision for its inclusion. In most cases, donated collections will be identified by bookplates and integrated into the collection.

CENSORSHIP

Libraries are often caught in the middle when it comes to the issue of censorship. The mission to support curriculum and selection criteria limits to some extent the scope and nature of the collection. Within this framework, however, care must be taken to allow free access to materials that might differ from, or be in opposition to, the doctrinal statement of the college.

A college library must be a forum for free exchange of ideas in the student's pursuit of knowledge and truth. With this in mind, the library will make available to its users materials offering the widest variety of viewpoint, regardless of their popularity or the popularity of the author or authors.

The library shall seek to provide materials representing the best spokesman in the areas, issues, or beliefs where there is honest disagreement.

Lastly, the library will base selection on the criteria stated above regardless of the controversial manner or language that an author may choose to use in dealing with subjects of religious, political, economic, scientific, philosophical, or moral issues.

Criticisms or attempts at censorship may be addressed through a "Request for Reconsideration" form. This form should be filled out and signed and submitted to the directory of library services. The complaint will be evaluated by the Library Committee. The action taken will be reported back to the individual filer of the complaint.

POLICY REVISION

This policy shall be reviewed on a biennial basis by the director of library services and/or professional staff. Revisions and additions may be made at that time.

Appendix J: Medical School "D" Library Policy

SELECTION AND ACQUISITION OF BOOKS:

Criteria and Implementation

I. Selection
   A. Language
      The library acquires only works entirely or mainly in English, with rare exceptions in cases of specific need.
   B. Content
      This statement reflects current policy and needs. The omission of a subject at the time of writing does not preclude its collectibility at a future date.
      1. Inclusions
         a. Clinical medicine, public health, and basic sciences (i.e., anatomy and genetics, biochemistry, pathology, etc.)
         b. History of medicine, including medical history and biography; medical iconography; reprints and facsimiles of medical classics; and translations of medical classics
         c. Hospital administration and related subjects

    d. Nursing (including psychiatric nursing) and history of nursing, excluding textbooks

    e. Psychiatry: only as the material is of general interest to the medical and nursing faculty and student body, or which deals with the medical and basic science aspects of psychiatry

    f. Social sciences relating to health care: delivery of health care; sociological or psychological studies of health problems; legal medicine; medical anthropology; medical ethics, rights of patients; social service, especially medical social service

    g. Bioengineering and computers in medicine

    h. Mathematics, limited chiefly to: biomathematics; biometrics (biostatistics); basic mathematics (limited number of titles)

    i. Organic, inorganic, and physical chemistry; physics. The library should have a basic collection of works in these fields (in addition, since several members of the Biochemistry Department work in the field of organic chemistry, new titles in this area should be referred and purchased as needed.)

    j. Reference material on a broad range of subjects

    k. Secondary areas: veterinary medicine and pathology (limited to a few standard texts); speech and hearing (excluding psychological aspects); language development, uses, function (especially in spoken medical communication); plant physiology, biochemistry, molecular chemistry, ultrastructure; culture of minorities in the United States (of interest to nursing students)

    l. Works by the Medical School "D" authors, or containing papers or chapters by the authors. (The former are purchased as a rule for both the Special Collection and circulation; the latter are purchased only for circulation.)

2. Limitations

The existence of several specialized libraries in the Medical Center makes it unnecessary for the library to strive for completeness in their areas. This library should purchase judiciously with reference to the purchasing policies of the other libraries as well as to the needs of the Medical School staff and student body. In some cases duplication is unavoidable. The wisest course is to keep in touch with the other librarians and to be aware of their acquisitions policy and practice. Other limitations are listed as follows:

      a. No popular medicine will be acquired except for personal accounts of illness and occasional best sellers (both fiction and nonfiction; but *no* popular diet books)

      b. British clinical texts in broad areas of medicine will be purchased only if they are outstanding new works or new editions of classic texts (Highly specialized clinical material and works in the basic sciences and on special subjects such as history of medicine or medical sociology and anthropology will be acquired according to the same criteria as U.S. publications.)

      c. Acquisitions in dentistry will include oral surgery and pathology, oral manifestations of systemic diseases, and a limited number of standard texts. (Dental specialties other than surgery will be excluded.)

      d. Psychology will not be collected except for child psychology bearing on child mental health

      e. Examination review books will be obtained only for the basic sciences and the broad specialties included in the clinical curriculum

3. Exclusions
   a. Undergraduate texts
   b. Popular books on diet
   c. Reprints from journals republished as monographs, i.e., complete issues or volumes of a single journal or collection of papers from various journals
   d. Workbooks with blanks for answers to be filled in by the reader, e.g., programmed texts

C. Quality

Excellence should be the goal of the selection process. It is, however, not always easy for the nonspecialist to recognize excellence, when even specialists will often disagree. The librarian will have to depend largely on superficial criteria, e.g.

1. Authors or editors: their reputation and affiliations
2. Edition number, if not the first edition; does the library have earlier editions and how much are they used?
3. Contributors: reputation and affiliations
4. If the book contains conference proceedings, the recency of the conference
5. Publisher's reputation
6. Preface and table of contents
7. Does the book have an index and is it sufficiently detailed?
8. Quality of illustrations and tables
9. Quality of book production: paper, print, binding

D. Usefulness

In clinical and research areas, the relevance of purchase to current needs is paramount. The need may be that of only one reader, but the need must exist. How well a field is represented in the library collection and how much the material is used is also to be considered. In less critical areas, where fewer titles are published while the usefulness of the individual title is more enduring, (e.g., history of medicine, personal accounts of illness, social sciences related to medicine, etc.) immediate need is less compelling, and worthwhile titles may be acquired, within budgetary limitations. If the selector is unsure of the usefulness of a particular title, the various aids for choosing consultants can be searched to disclose activity in a given research or clinical area; books may be referred if doubt persists.

E. Costs

Unless the price is totally beyond reason, a book should not be rejected solely because of cost. Cost should be the deciding factor where the need for the book itself is in question. All books, the cost of which seems disproportionate to their content, should be referred. Most consultants are quite sensitive to the cost factor in their evaluation of library material. *Please note*: All single titles costing over $100.00 must be approved by the Librarian.

II. Aids to selection

A. Approval shipments

B. Published information

1. Publishers' announcements and advertisements in journals
2. Book lists
   a. National Library of Medicine proofsheets
   b. *Weekly Record*
   c. Acquisitions lists from other libraries
   d. *Monthly Catalog of U.S. Government Publications*
   e. Selected U.S. government publications
   f. "New Books Received" columns in journals, e.g., *Science, American Journal of Nursing*
3. Book Reviews

   In most cases, books considered for purchase by the Medical School "D" Library are too recently published to have been reviewed in the scientific press. Nevertheless the book review section of a selected group of journals should be regularly perused because, regardless of the publication date of the title discussed, a good review is often a distillation of valuable information on an unfamiliar subject. In addition, a review may call attention to a title that has been overlooked, or, if it appears in a British journal, that has not yet been issued in the United States. The book review sections of the popular press should also be examined regularly for substantial titles in the health field issued by trade and university presses.

C. Referrals

Books should be referred if their subject matter is not within the selector's area of competence, and the selector is in doubt concerning their essential merit, their usefulness to the staff of the Medical Center, and their cost, i.e., the ratio of cost to usefulness. Books may be referred to one or more faculty consultants, depending on the number of disciplines dealt within them. Collective volumes, especially proceedings, which are essentially unscreened and unedited material, should be referred. Titles should be referred to the specific individuals who are active in the areas covered by the books in question. Should it be unclear whether a book on a specific clinical or research aspect is relevant to the activity of the Center, certain local publications should be consulted: (1) the catalog of the Medical School; (2) the catalog of the Graduate School of Medical Sciences; (3) the catalog of fourth-year electives; (4) the catalog of the School of Nursing; and (5) the annual reports of the Society and of other institutions affiliated with the Medical Center. Curiosity and imagination are needed to ferret out the potential sources that will yield information; these sources include people as well as print.

D. Readers' recommendations

Faculty members, students, research technicians, nurses, and other staff members are encouraged to suggest titles for purchase. Their requests should, however, be carefully reviewed before being acted upon. It is helpful to discuss the suggestion with the reader to find out why the book has been recommended, if the reason is not obvious. If the request falls within the limits of appropriateness for the library it should be accepted; if not, it should be rejected, and the reader should be informed of the reason for rejection.

E. Interlibrary loan requests

Interlibrary loan files are an indicator of the gaps in the library collection. They may indicate areas that the library deliberately de-emphasizes. On the other hand, they may reveal vulnerable points that should be strengthened as soon as possible. The file of interlibrary loan requests should be regularly reviewed at stated intervals.

F. Class reserve lists
    Titles needed for class reserves are routed to the Acquisitions
    Department after being screened by the Circulation Depart-
    ment. Titles are purchased for class reserve if the library has
    no copy already or has an insufficient number of copies. The
    circulation librarian decides how many copies of a particular
    item are to be purchased. If a publication is to be used by 100
    students at least three copies should be bought. If books are
    available in inexpensive editions, as many as six copies per
    100 students may be obtained. If the reading assignment con-
    sists of a relatively small number of pages (e.g., one or two
    chapters), photocopies of the requisite pages are made instead
    of multiple copies of the book being bought. The acquisitions
    librarian must evaluate purchases in terms of the availability
    of funds. When funds are insufficient to meet current needs,
    the director must be advised.

Appendix K: Weekly Interview Instrument

1. How did you determine what needs were to be filled in the collections this week?
2. How did you identify which titles to order this week?
3. Did you identify titles for purchase from sources other than those regularly scanned?
4. Were there any titles originally selected by you which were then rejected for purchase? If yes, why?
5. Were there any timing problems with regard to sending out orders for materials for the collections?
6. How did you decide to not order many of the titles about which you read during the past week?
7. What titles did you discard this week?
8. With what interruptions did you have to contend while trying to select materials for purchase?

Bibliography

Accreditation Manual for Hospitals. Chicago, IL: Joint Commission on Accreditation for Hospitals, 1986.

American Association of School Librarians; Association for Educational Communications and Technology. *Information Power: Guidelines for School Library Media Programs.* Chicago: American Library Association; Washington, DC: AECT, 1988.

American Library Association. *Guidelines for Collection Development.* Chicago: American Library Association, 1979.

Archer, Earnest R. "How to Make a Business Decision: An Analysis of Theory and Practice." *Management Review* 69 (February 1980): 54–61.

Atkinson, Ross. "The Language of the Levels: Reflections on the Communication of Collection Development Policy." *College & Research Libraries* 47 (March 1986): 140–149.

Bailey, Janet D. "New Journal Decision Making." *College & Research Libraries* 50 (May 1989): 354–359.

Bass, Bernard M. *Organizational Decision Making.* Homewood, IL: Richard D. Irwin, 1983.

Baughman, James C. "Toward a Structural Approach to Collection

Development." *College & Research Libraries* 38 (May 1977): 241–248.

Becker, Karen A. "CD-ROM: A Primer." *College & Research Libraries News* 48 (July/August 1987): 388–393.

Bensman, Stephen J. "Journal Collection Management as a Cumulative Advantage Process." *College & Research Libraries* 46 (January 1985): 13–29.

Bostic, Mary J. "A Written Collection Development Policy: To Have and Have Not." *Collection Management* 10 (1988): 89–103.

Boyce, Bert R., and Pollens, Janet Sue. "Citation-Based Impact Measures and the Bradfordian Selection Criteria." *Collection Management* 4 (Fall 1982): 29–36.

Broadus, Robert N. "On Citations, Uses, and Informed Guesswork: A Response to Line." *College & Research Libraries* 46 (January 1985): 38–39.

———. "A Proposed Method for Eliminating Titles From Periodical Subscription Lists." *College & Research Libraries* 46 (January 1985): 30–35.

Clapp, Verner W., and Jordan, Robert T. "Quantitative Criteria for Adequacy of Academic Library Collections." *College & Research Libraries* 26 (September 1965): 371–380.

Coughlin, Ellen K. "IRS Ruling is Seen Threatening Supplies of Many Scholarly and Professional Books." *The Chronicle of Higher Education* 21 (September 29, 1980): 1, 22.

Crowe, Lawson, and Anthes, Susan H. "The Academic Librarian and Information Technology: Ethical Issues." *College & Research Libraries* 49 (March 1988): 123–130.

Dahlin, Robert. "Learning to Live With Thor." *Publishers Weekly* 221 (March 5, 1982): 26–29.

———. "Thor: How Hard Will the Hammer Fall?" *Publishers Weekly* 218 (December 26, 1980): 28–32.

DePew, John N. "An Acquisitions Decision Model for Academic Libraries." *Journal of the American Society for Information Science* 26 (July/August 1975): 237–246.

Elementary School Library Collection: A Guide to Books and Other Media. 16th ed. Ed. by Lois Winkel. Williamsport, PA: Brodart, 1988.

Evans, G. Edward. *Developing Library and Information Center Collections.* 2nd ed. Littleton, CO: Libraries Unlimited, 1987.

Farrell, David, and Reed-Scott, Jutta. "The North American Collections Inventory Project: Implications for the Future of Coordinated Management of Research Collections." *Library Resources & Technical Services* 33 (January 1989): 15–28.

Feiner, Arlene M. "Frameworking in Cooperative Collection Development." *Illinois Libraries* 71 (January 1989): 25–31.

Ferguson, Anthony W., Grant, Joan, and Rutstein, Joel S. "The RLG Conspectus: Its Uses and Benefits." *College & Research Libraries* 49 (May 1988): 197–206.

Fischel, Daniel N. "Thor's Seldgehammer Blow Against Books . . . The Case for Repealing a Tax Law." *Publishers Weekly* 218 (August 1, 1980): 17–18.

Foti, Laura. "CD-I: A Focal Technology." *CD-ROM Librarian* 2 (May 1988): 21–24.

Genaway, David C. "PBA: Percentage Based Allocation for Acquisitions: A Simplified Method for the Allocation of the Library Materials Budget." *Library Acquisitions: Practice & Theory* 10 (1986): 287–292.

———. "The Q Formula: The Flexible Formula for Library Acquisitions in Relation to the FTE Driven Formula." *Library Acquisitions: Practice & Theory* 10 (1986): 293–306.

Gordon, Lawrence A., Miller, Danny, and Mintzberg, Henry. *Normative Models in Managerial Decision-Making.* New York: National Association of Accountants, 1975.

Goss, Theresa C. "Middle-Management Participatory Decision Making." *Community & Junior College Libraries* 3 (Fall 1984): 35–41.

Grannis, Chandler B. "Book Title Output and Average Prices: 1987 Preliminary Figures." In *The Bowker Annual of Library and Book Trade Information* pp. 402–412. 33rd ed. New York: Bowker, 1988.

Gwinn, Nancy E., and Mosher, Paul H. "Coordinating Collection Development: The RLG Conspectus." *College & Research Libraries* 44 (March 1980): 128–140.

Hazen, Dan C. "Knowledge, Information Transactions, Collection Growth, and Model Building: Some Not-Quite-Random Thoughts." *Cornell University Library Bulletin* 212 (1979): 11–15.

Heirs, Ben, with Farrell, Peter. *The Professional Decision-Thinker: Our New Management Priority.* London: Sidgwick & Jackson, 1986.

Heirs, Ben, and Pehrson, Gordon. *The Mind of the Organization: On the Relevance of the Decision-Thinking Processes of the Human Mind to the Decision-Thinking Processes of Organizations.* New York: Harper & Row, 1972.

Hodges, Gerald G. "Decision-Making for Young Adult Services in Public Libraries." *Library Trends* 37 (Summer 1988): 106–114.

Intner, Sheila S. "Responsibilities of Technical Service Librarians to the Process of Collection Evaluation." *Library Trends* 22 (Winter 1985): 417–436.

Jacobson, Susan D. "Comments." *Library Acquisitions: Practice & Theory* 10 (1986): 307–309.

Jaramillo, George R. "Computer Technology and Its Impact on Collection Development." *Collection Management* 10 (1988): 1–13.

Kovacs, Beatrice. "Decision-Making in Collection Development: Medical School Libraries." D.L.S. diss., Columbia University, 1983.

Lancaster, F. W. "Electronic Publishing." *Library Trends* 37 (Winter 1989): 316–325.

———. "Evaluating Collections by Their Use." *Collection Management* 4 (Spring/Summer 1982): 15–43.

Leigh, Andrew. *Decisions, Decisions! A Practical Management Guide to Problem Solving and Decision Making.* Brookfield, VT: Gower Publishing Co., 1983.

Lein, Edward. "Suggestions for Formulating Collection Development Policy Statements for Music Score Collections in Academic Libraries." *Collection Management* 9 (Winter 1987): 69–89.

Lenzini, Rebecca T. "Prices of U.S. and Foreign Published Materials." In *The Bowker Annual of Library and Book Trade Information*, pp. 424–444, 33rd ed. New York: Bowker, 1988.

Lewis, David W. "Inventing the Electronic University." *College & Research Libraries* 49 (July 1988): 291–305.

"Librarians Beware!" *MLA News* 143 (March 1982): 5.

Line, Maurice B. "Use of Citation Data for Periodicals Control in Libraries: A Response to Broadus." *College & Research Libraries* 45 (January 1985): 36–37.

Lockman, Edward J. "Is the Customer Always Right; or Wait a Minute, Don't You Want My Business? (Publishing Policies and Their Impact on Markets)." *Library Acquisitions: Practice & Theory* 11 (1987): 121–123.

Loe, Mary H. "*Thor* Tax Ruling After 5 Years: Its Effect on Publishing and Libraries." *Library Acquisitions: Practice & Theory* 10 (1986): 203–218.

Loertscher, David V. "Collection Mapping: An Evaluation Strategy for Collection Development." *Drexel Library Quarterly* 21 (Spring 1985): 9–21.

———. "The Elephant Technique of Collection Development." *Collection Management* 7 (Fall/Winter 1985/86): 45–54.

Loertscher, David V., and Ho, May Lein. *Computerized Collection Development for School Library Media Centers.* Excellence in School Library Media Programs, No. 2. Fayetteville, AK: Hi Willow Research and Publishing (P.O. Box 1801), 1986.

Losee, Robert M., Jr. "A Decision Theoretic Model of Materials Selection for Acquisition." *Library Quarterly* 57 (July 1987): 269–283.

McCall, Morgan W., Jr., and Kaplan, Robert E. *Whatever It Takes: Decision Makers At Work.* Englewood Cliffs, NJ: Prentice-Hall, 1985.

McGrath, William E. "Multidimensional Mapping of Book Circulation in a University Library." *College & Research Libraries* 42 (March 1983): 103–115.

McInnis, R. Marvin. "The Formula Approach to Library Size: An Empirical Study of Its Efficacy Evaluating Research Libraries." *College & Research Libraries* 33 (May 1972): 190–198.

Melcher, Arlyn J. *Structure and Process of Organizations: A Systems Approach.* Englewood Cliffs, NJ: Prentice-Hall, 1976.

Metz, Paul, and Litchfield, Charles A. "Measuring Collections Use at Virginia Tech." *College & Research Libraries* 49 (November 1988): 501–513.

Millson-Martula, Christopher A. "The Greater Midwest Regional Medical Library Network and Coordinated Cooperative Collection Development: The RLG Conspectus and Beyond." *Illinois Libraries* 71 (January 1989): 31–39.

Mintzberg, Henry. "Planning on the Left Side and Managing on the Right." *Harvard Business Review* 54 (July/August 1976): 49–58.

Mintzberg, Henry, Raisinghani, Duru, and Théorêt, André. "The Structure of 'Unstructured' Decision Processes." *Administrative Science Quarterly* 21 (June 1976): 246–275.

Mosher, Paul H. "Quality and Library Collections: New Directions in Research and Practice in Collection Evaluation." *Advances in Librarianship* 13 (1984): 211–238.

Mulliner, Kent. "The Acquisitions Allocation Formula at Ohio University." *Library Acquisitions: Practice & Theory* 10 (1986): 315–327.

Murray, William, et al. "Collection Mapping and Collection Development." *Drexel Library Quarterly* 21 (Spring 1985): 40–51.

Newcomb, J. "Electronic Information Distribution: The Role of the Traditional Publisher and the Librarian." *Special Libraries* 74 (April 1983): 150–155.

Nielsen, Brian. "The Second Annual CD-ROM Expo: The Latest in the Technology." *CD-ROM Librarian* 3 (November/December 1988): 14–18.

Nissley, Meta. "Optical Technology: Considerations for Collection Development." *Library Acquisitions: Practice & Theory* 12 (1988): 11–15.

Oberg, Larry R. "Evaluating the Conspectus Approach for Smaller Library Collections." *College & Research Libraries* 49 (May 1988): 187–196.

Palais, Elliot. "Use of Course Analysis in Compiling a Collection Development Policy Statement for a University Library." *Journal of Academic Librarianship* 13 (March 1987): 8–13.

Raffel, Jeffrey A. "From Economic to Political Analysis of Library Decision Making." *College & Research Libraries* 35 (November 1974): 412–423.

Raiffa, Howard. *Decision Analysis: Introductory Lectures on Choices Under Uncertainty*. Reading, MA: Addison-Wesley, 1968.

Resnick, Michael D. *Choices: An Introduction to Decision Theory*. Minneapolis: Univ. of Minnesota Press, 1987.

Sanders, Nancy P., O'Neill, Edward T., and Weibel, Stuart L. "Automated Collection Analysis Using the OCLC and RLG Bibliographic Databases." *College & Research Libraries* 49 (July 1988): 305–314.

Sandler, Mark. "Quantitative Approaches to Qualitative Collection Assessment." *Collection Building* 8 (1988): 12–17.

Schmidt, Karen A. " 'Never Read Any Book That Is Not a Year Old': Thor Power Tool, the Publishing Industry, and Library Collections." *Technical Services Quarterly* 2 (Spring/Summer 1985): 93–101.

Schrift, Leonard. "After Thor, What's Next: The Thor Power Tool Decision (US Supreme Court) and Its Impact on Scholarly Publishing." *Library Acquisitions: Practice and Theory* 9 (1985): 61–63.

Sellen, Mary. "Book Budget Formula Allocations: A Review Essay." *Collection Management* 9 (Winter 1987): 13–24.

Senghas, Dorothy, and Warro, Edward A. "Book Allocations: The Key to a Plan for Collection Development." *Library Acquisitions: Practice & Theory* 6 (1982): 47–53.

Shad, Jasper G. "Fairness in Book Fund Allocation." *College & Research Libraries* 48 (November 1987): 479–486.

Simon, Herbert A. *Administrative Behavior: A Study of Decision-Making Process in Administrative Organization*. 3rd. ed. New York: Free Press, 1976.

Sowell, Steven L. "Expanding Horizons on Collection Development With Expert Systems: Development and Testing of a Demonstration Prototype." *Special Libraries* 80 (Winter 1989): 45–50.

Standera, Oldrich. *The Electronic Era of Publishing: An Overview of Concepts, Technologies and Methods*. New York: Elsevier, 1987.

Stankus, Tony, and Rice, Barbara. "Handle With Care: Use and Citation Data for Science Journal Management." *Collection Management* 4 (Spring/Summer 1982): 95–110.

Stephenson, Mary Sue, and Purcell, Gary R. "Application of Systems Analysis to Depository Library Decision Making Regarding the Use of New Technology." *Government Information Quarterly* 1 (1984): 285–307.

Thor Power Tool Co. v. Commissioner of Internal Revenue, 439 U.S. 522–550, 1979.

Watson, Peter G. "Collection Development and Evaluation in Reference and Adult Services Librarianship." *RQ* 26 (Winter 1986): 143–145.

Welsch, Erwin K. "Back to the Future: A Personal Statement on Collection Development in an Information Culture." *Library Resources & Technical Services* 33 (January 1989): 29–36.

Wheeler, Daniel D., and Janis, Irving L. *A Practical Guide for Making Decisions*. New York: Free Press, 1980.

Wiberley, Stephen E., Jr. "Journal Rankings From Citation Studies: A Comparison of National and Local Data From Social Work." *Library Quarterly* 52 (October 1982): 348–359.

Index

About the Author

BEATRICE KOVACS is Assistant Professor, Department of Library and Information Studies, School of Education, at the University of North Carolina, Greensboro. She is the author of *Health Sciences Librarianship: A Guide to Information Sources.*